Combat A

DUCKWORTH DEBATES IN ARCHAEOLOGY

Series editor: Richard Hodges

Also available

Combat Archaeology

MATERIAL CULTURE AND
MODERN CONFLICT

John Schofield

Duckworth

First published in 2005 by
Gerald Duckworth & Co. Ltd.
90-93 Cowcross Street, London EC1M 6BF
Tel: 020 7490 7300
Fax: 020 7490 0080
inquiries@duckworth-publishers.co.uk
www.ducknet.co.uk

A catalogue record for this book is available
from the British Library

ISBN 0 7156 3403 8

Typeset by Ray Davies
Printed and bound in Great Britain by
CPI, Bath

Contents

For Armorel and James

Illustrations

Figures

Tables

Preface

There are several reasons why I wrote this book, conscious that there are other published works that describe the archaeology of recent conflict far better than I can. It was written to meet very particular demands, realised during my teaching of heritage management at the University of Southampton, and lectures in Australia and the United States in 2000-03. This, combined with an involvement over ten years with the developing field of contemporary archaeology, caused me to think more about social contexts, and the values attributed to military remains, rather than merely their survival and physical form which are quite understandably the focus of most published works. I wanted to explore the close connections felt towards modern military sites, and more specifically the rationale behind them: why do people want their local pillbox preserved; why do veterans return to the airfields from which they flew; and why does the survival of a ruined control tower complement that experience, that sense of place? I wanted to begin to develop a social and theoretical context for the archaeological remains of recent conflict.

The book follows a logical progression that conforms approximately to what is generally referred to in heritage management terms as the 'management cycle'. It addresses in turn: what is the material culture of modern warfare; why does it matter and to whom; how can it be either protected or taken account of when threatened with development, for example; and how can the surviving sites be presented and interpreted for public enjoyment and benefit. It provides an overview; a synopsis in some areas, but always referencing further studies, of which many now exist. This book does not claim to be definitive in any sense. Rather, like other books in this series, it raises issues of concern and controversy, and presents them in such a way as to provoke thought and consideration in others.

As well as being a book about the social archaeology of warfare and conflict, it also represents a study in archaeology and the modern world more generally. It addresses issues such as the relevance of archaeology and archaeological theory, methods and approaches towards the recent past and the contemporary world. In the words of Buchli and Lucas (2001), it contributes to an emerging and diverse literature which addresses this point, seeking to make the familiar unfamiliar. As well as being a review of ideas, theories and examples relating to modern warfare, it also serves as a case study in how to treat the modern world through an archaeological approach, and more specifically how to manage this recent material culture.

The book relies on personal experience, both from my management of and involvement with projects commissioned by English Heritage, and from my own research. Thus, some obvious areas are under-represented, such as the Boer War, for example, which marks the start of the modern period I refer to. Other subjects are perhaps over-represented, such as the Cold War. But often it is these later examples which present the greatest challenges for interpretation and heritage management, so the focus may be justified in those terms at least. Some examples have appeared elsewhere, notably the interpretations cited in Chapter 5, which are also outlined in Schofield (in press).

I am indebted to David Hunt and William Gray Johnson for their assistance and advice in bringing this text to completion. David's expertise has been invaluable, correcting errors and suggesting interesting and significant new avenues to pursue.

Bill I have known for some years. Much of his work has involved recording Cold War remains in the Nevada Desert, and latterly as Director of the new museum in Las Vegas built to interpret the State's Cold War heritage. Like David, Bill has given his time generously, offering suggestions and ideas that have greatly improved the volume's scope and depth. I would also like to thank all those colleagues – both within and beyond English Heritage – who have given support, expert advice and friendship over the years, in particular Wayne Cocroft, Jeremy Lake and Roger J.C. Thomas. The book will I hope be a testament to the co-operative and collegiate working relationships we and others have developed. I am grateful also to Vince Griffin of English Heritage for producing Figures 1.1, 3.1 and 4.1 from my scribbled originals, Lucy Orta and Jason Evans for permission to use the cover illustration and Figure 2.1, Darwin Morgan and the US Department of Energy for permission to use Figure 1.2, Keith Angus for Figure 2.4, and English Heritage for Figure 4.2.

This book has been produced in difficult times, and my greatest debt is to Armorel and James for their support, patience and generosity over the past two years. The book is for them.

1

Characterising combat archaeology

Archaeologists typically engage new periods by first examining evidence for warfare and conflict, taking note of military arte-facts and architecture, before moving onto other themes and topics. Perhaps this is because there is something captivating and compelling about warfare, and why people fight. Perhaps it is because for some periods the material culture of war and conflict is the most obvious; the most monumental. Perhaps it is simply that archaeologists in the past have often had military training, or a military career, and are thereby attracted to the familiar. Or perhaps it is because the research questions relating to war and conflict are among the most interesting, challenging or controversial to face. For whatever reason, archaeologists studying the medieval period began with castles; studies of the Roman period began with forts; and the archaeology of the modern period has started with its military-industrial legacy, albeit more broadly defined than merely the places where conflict occurred.

Since archaeologists first took an interest in the material remains of modern warfare (e.g. Wills 1985), much has been achieved. In recent years in particular the subject has been increasingly taken up by professional researchers and heritage practitioners, in equal measure and with great enthusiasm (e.g. Cocroft and Thomas 2003; Dobinson 2000a, 2001; Saunders 2004; Schofield et al. 2002; Schofield 2004 for a summary). The increasingly post-modern, multi-vocal and trans-disciplinary approach to these studies of modern warfare have also reflected a wider trend, towards integration or 'consilience' where – the renowned biologist E.O. Wilson claims (2001) – the greatest benefits to research lie. Modern military studies have started to explore the potential for crossing established disciplinary boundaries. Addison and Crang's *Burning Blue: a new history of the Battle of Britain* (2000) demonstrates how diverse experiences of an event or historical episode can bring new insight and colour to what many considered a familiar past. Saunders' (2004) overview of World War I brings together historians, archaeologists, anthropologists, sociologists and geographers to re-evaluate meaning and the social and cultural significance of the conflict. And there have been other trends to emerge, such as the flurry of recent studies into the origins of conflict (e.g. various papers in Carman 1997; Hill and Wileman 2002, 15ff.). In general the archaeology of modern conflict has now developed into a subject area that typically draws upon historical accounts and reviews (e.g. Keegan 1995), historical geography (e.g. Landzelius 2003), politics (Gaddis 1997), political geography (e.g. Charlesworth 1994) and social historical research (e.g. Bourke 1999) to give context to the studies of material culture where archaeologies of modern conflict more conventionally begin.

This book will consider why archaeologists are interested in the modern period, and specifically the material remains of recent warfare and conflict, and why there is such enthusiasm within this aspect of modern material culture studies to cross disciplinary boundaries. It also provides a case study in cultural resource management, exploring the related issues of significance, protection, management and interpretation.

What are presented here are personal views, however, and views some will disagree with. The approach taken follows some recent anthropological studies that emphasise social significance and values (Byrne et al. 2001), and which examine past events in a rather personal, intimate and engaging way (e.g. Read 1996). But that's one of the benefits of studying this modern period from an archaeological perspective: we are dealing with the familiar, and with what the material culture of the familiar means to us, as a profession, as a society, as a cultural group within society, and as individuals. This book is a review of thoughts, ideas and approaches; methods and motivations. It is intended to provoke responses among archaeologists and those concerned with material culture and cultural resource management, and to encourage others to engage with it; to think beyond the concrete (pill)box, and examine the wider social relevance of this particular sub-set of modern material culture. This is a post-modern narrative therefore, recognising the multiplicity of views and interpretations, but recognising the relevance and validity of all.

Purpose

Warfare is unavoidably and inevitably part of our lives. We experience it, witness it, and learn about it to varying degrees. Some of us who study the recent past are related to soldiers, sailors or airmen, or those involved in research and development for military purposes, or in an industry that supports the military in some way. We watch films and documentaries and read books on the subject. We follow news accounts of wars around the world, read of atrocities in our newspapers, and watch scenes unfold on television. Some accept war as a necessary evil, while others protest actively against it. Some participate in acts of remembrance; others would rather forget. And independent of all these interests, a few of us are involved with the material culture of war, promoting people's understanding of it and advocating recording, research or preservation efforts where appropriate. Heritage managers and researchers believe this material culture can be used to recall defining moments of the twentieth century, as happened in 1994 on the Normandy beaches, and again in 2004, ten years later. Others regard modern military archaeology as conveying cautionary tales; lessons for the future, describing these places more for their discord (Dolff-Bonekaemper nd) or dissonance (Tunbridge and Ashworth 1997) values; for being a 'heritage that hurts' (Uzzell 1989).

Throughout, this book will explore perceptions, attitudes and approaches to the archaeology of modern warfare. After a general introduction, it first describes the material (*matériel*) culture of modern warfare (Chapter 2). Chapter 3 outlines the relevance and meaning of this evidence, placing it within the wider context of an emerging archaeology of the modern period. It asks the questions: What are the benefits of this archaeology of the recent past? What does it tell us that we wouldn't otherwise know? I will then examine the means by which this resource can be managed and in some cases protected to best effect (Chapter 4), and how it can be presented and interpreted (Chapter 5). Examples that I consider in depth are comparatively few, preferring instead to return to a selection of case studies from the different perspectives that each chapter provides. Examples are also fully referenced, so that those who wish to can explore them in more detail than space allows here.

As the title indicates, this is not a book exclusively about war, in the sense of front-line combat. It takes as its theme the archaeology of warfare and conflict in its broadest sense, and notably the social archaeology of all that supports armed forces at war, or training or preparing for war, in deterrence, or performing other civil duties related to the war effort, seeking to minimise the effects of war on the population. This book concerns the families of combatants, the industries that support militarism, those that oppose it, and those affected by it directly (e.g. those most affected by the Blitz or by environmental pollution created by nuclear industry in the American Midwest [e.g. Kuletz 1998]). It also covers civil conflict. In other words it is a broad social archaeology of conflict (Gilchrist 2003), just as much as it is explicitly militaristic in scope.

This first chapter outlines some of the characteristics of modern warfare and conflict. First it defines what we mean by modern warfare, before looking at what sets it apart from what came before, and what is likely to come after. It outlines the role of archaeology, and describes the type of archaeology it is. A key point is that any attempt to define archaeology of warfare and conflict is unavoidably politicised and theorised according to the author's cultural background, and the environment in which s/he operates, personally and professionally. However objective one tries to be, a former soldier, sailor or airman now practising professional archaeology will inevitably view military archaeology differently from a former peace activist in the same role (and both situations do exist within British archaeology!). There is another point. Any archaeology of the modern period will be personalised to a degree; it will represent almost by definition an archaeology of us, providing the opportunity to assess our own society from within, as a critique on modern life (Graves Brown 2000). And this book pursues that line as a kind of sub-text. As well as having cultural benefit for all, this archaeology of modern conflict is also an intimate archaeology of ourselves, of how we study the past and how we react to it. The archaeology of modern conflict is important for both of these reasons, and examples later in the book emphasise this point.

The twentieth century – warfare in an 'age of extremes'

It was the socialist historian Eric Hobsbawn that defined the twentieth century as an age of extremes (1995). And it was other eminent historians, philosophers and commentators that gave colour to that statement in the notes accompanying his book. William Golding described the twentieth century as 'the most violent', and Isaiah Berlin 'the most terrible' in Western history. Severo Ochoa, the Spanish scientist, noted how 'the progress of science' is the most fundamental thing, a point with which Raymond Firth agreed: 'Technologically, I single out the development of electronics among the most significant ... of the twentieth century.' All these statements are undoubtedly true, and with time many of these characteristics will surely merge into some generic description of a Technological (or Information Technological) Age (Rogers 1999). Research and Development (R&D), for example, underpins much scientific progress and advancement, including improved communications and artificial intelligence, and the speed with which information can be relayed around the world. It has also had a significant role in the development of weapons and defence-related technology – for example, radar in the 1930s; guided weapons systems during the Cold War; and internet technology, strategically important for military use as it ensures that messages can find their way through damaged networks, as well as enabling dispersed groups to communicate.

It is true that these developments, and their implications, have set twentieth-century warfare apart, both from what came before and most probably from what will follow. But recent warfare is different in other ways too, notably in terms of its accessibility. While only a minority among us will have taken up arms or been present within theatres of war, access to the media, and the availability of real-time live coverage, often from the front-line, makes us all witnesses; if not actually first-hand then virtually so. For all these reasons, and because of the availability of matériel culture (as Chapter 2 will outline), the significance of primary and oral historical sources, and the ability to review these sources critically, this is a fascinating area for archaeological research, made all the more so by its

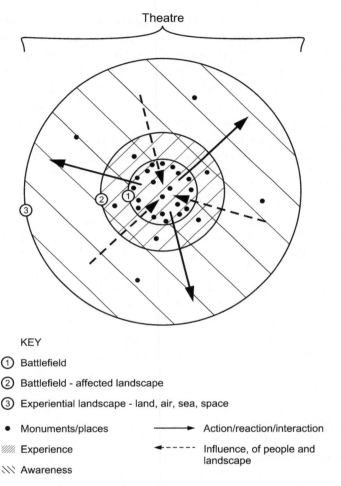

Fig. 1.1. The theatre of war.

close proximity and by our personal experiences of conflict, albeit usually filtered through the media.

Warfare and conflict are broadly defined for the purpose of this volume. It covers all conflict, whether primarily military or civil, from smaller-scale ethnic disputes, to larger civil conflicts such as those occurring in the former Eastern Europe and Africa for instance, to the World Wars and the Cold War. It also recognises the size and complexity of the theatre in which warfare is conducted (Figure 1.1), taking in battlefields and the wider landscape directly affected by war, and the landscape of experience which is more significant for the influence it had on events on the battlefield than necessarily being a part of the battlefield itself. For terrestrial battlefields, this experiential landscape often includes the sea, the air, and space, such a significant new frontier so far as the Cold War was concerned (Gorman 2005).

The definition of conflict used for this book therefore includes the conflict itself, people's experience of it, and the material culture that relates to that engagement, whether installations such as coast batteries, radar stations and anti-aircraft gun sites; aircraft, armoured fighting vehicles and vessels; personal effects such as domestic architecture and possessions; or people's experiences conveyed as words, voices or pictures. All this material contributes to the archaeology of modern warfare and will be discussed in the chapters that follow.

Context

To provide context for that material record, this section will briefly examine some of the characteristics of twentieth-century warfare, notably: speed; techniques, technology and accuracy; scale; alliances; and reporting and representation. Following his initial interest in warfare, expressed in *Bunker Archeology* (1991), all of these themes have been the subject of review by the theorist and philosopher Paul Virilio (see e.g. [with Lotringer] 1997; 2002; Gane 1999 for a review of his work and influence), whose work forms much of the basis for the discussions that follow.

1. Characterising combat archaeology

Speed

Virilio has written much on the significance of speed in under-standing modern warfare (Virilio and Lotringer 1997; Virilio 2002). He has noted how the speed of decision-making is reflex-ive of emerging technology: in the nineteenth century battles unfolded over days, and decision-making and response times could be measured in hours. The Boer War (1899-1902) is an example of the slower pace of conflict, with horses, balloons, steam traction engines, long marches, sieges and armoured trains. In World War II this came down to the few minutes between enemy aircraft appearing on early warning radar, and being engaged by anti-aircraft artillery and intercept aircraft. In the Cold War the significance of the three-minute warning is well documented, these warnings and practice sirens either an all-too-recent memory (although those I consulted, and who lived through the Cold War, couldn't recall whether it was three or four minutes!) or instead deeply ingrained through its use in popular culture. Reflecting this degree of instancy, Virilio and Lotringer wrote:

> We no longer have time for reflection. The power of speed is *that*. Democracy is that. Democracy is no longer in the hands of men, it's in the hands of computerised instru-ments and answering machines etc. Today there is still reaction time. It was approximately half an hour in 1961. Andropov and Reagan have no more than several minutes (1997, 61).

Even over ten years, between the first Gulf War and the second, response times have changed significantly, from seconds to nano-seconds, as communications networks continue to im-prove. Virilio refers to weapons of instantaneous communica-

21

tion, available thanks to the development of globalised news networks and telesurveillance (2002, 49).

Speed can also be traced in the technology of weapons systems and the ability of armoured fighting vehicles, aircraft and ships to operate within these increasingly sophisticated environments. World War II weapons were more sophisticated than those of World War I, for example; aircraft were faster, and detection systems were increasingly sophisticated as a result. Laser technology and satellites now have the capacity to deliver an immediate impact. The material record – artefacts and places – provides the physical manifestation of these developments. (Books on explosives [Cocroft 2000] and the Cold War [Cocroft and Thomas 2003] contain examples of the impact of speed on the material culture of warfare and combat.)

Techniques, technology and accuracy

Virilio identifies three major epochs of war (2002, 6-7): the tactical and prehistorical epoch, consisting of limited violence and confrontations; the strategic epoch, historical and purely political; and the contemporary and transpolitical logistical epoch, where, 'science and industry play a determining role in the destructive power of opposing forces' (ibid.). Within this framework can be seen the development of weaponry and its increasing significance alongside a specific 'mode of deterrence'. In the first period, weapons of obstruction predominate (ditches and ramparts; armour), linked closely to the practice of siege warfare; then came weapons of destruction (lances, bows, artillery and machine-guns) which represented a war of movement; and finally 'real-time' weapons of communication (information and transport, wireless telephone, radar and satellites) that represent blitzkrieg, or total war (Table 1.1).

These developments can be traced into the twentieth century, with many of the weapons and delivery systems now well

1. Characterising combat archaeology

Epoch	Characteristics	Type of warfare	Weaponry
Tactical and prehistorical PREHISTORY	Limited violence and confrontations	Siege	Weapons of obstruction (ditches, ramparts, armour)
Strategic MEDIEVAL	Historical and purely political	Movement	Weapons of destruction (lances, bows, artillery, machine guns)
Contemporary and transpolitical/ logistical MODERN	Science and industry	Total war	Weapons of communication (information, transport, telephone, radar, satellites)

Table 1.1. The ages of war (1) (after Virilio 2002).

known through media reports and popular culture. The materials used to wage trench warfare in World War I, for example, are well documented (see various papers in Saunders 2004), as are those of World War II and the Cold War. Rocket technology emerged in World War II through the development of the V1 and V2 unmanned weapons, used to attack British targets. After the war some of the same scientists put this experience to use in developing British and American rocket technology (e.g. Cocroft 2000, 248). Blue Streak was Britain's Cold War rocket programme, given high political priority in the 1950s, and intended to be an intercontinental ballistic missile delivery system for Britain's independent nuclear deterrent (ibid., 255-61). Sites were constructed for testing the various components, including for live firing at Woomera in South Australia. But in 1960, even before some of the facilities were completed, the Blue Streak programme was cancelled. It was thought to be vulnerable to pre-emptive strike by the Soviet Union, and there was a need to reduce defence expenditure. And that is often the way with developing technology, and with Research and Development. Programmes will be realigned, intensified or cancelled depending on their success, the promise shown in early stages of work, developments within science and technology more generally, and the wider political agenda. From an archaeological point of view many of these various related programmes remain to be studied, and sometimes without the available archives and oral historical evidence (but cf. Walley 2001 for an example of what oral history can contribute where those most closely involved are able to describe their experiences).

With time weapons generally continue to become smarter, quicker and more accurate, inevitably reducing the scope for reaction time. Accuracy has great significance, as it allows an attack to be more strategic, more focused. It can also reduce the chance of civilian casualties (though accidents still occur). The first and second Gulf Wars demonstrated how targets can be sought out precisely, and then hit with virtually no prior warning. Improvements in technology and the accuracy of weapons systems also impact on the sophistication of decoy and deception. The use of decoys in World War II, in the form of dummy targets and camouflage, is now well documented (e.g. Dobinson 2000a). The build-up of an allied invasion force in the UK in advance of D-Day made effective use of both techniques, by hiding troops and matériel in woodland close to the embarkation ports, and posting dummy aircraft and vehicles in East Anglia to draw the eyes of enemy reconnaissance. This was Operation *Fortitude*, now one of the most intensively studied strategic operations of World War II (Dobinson 2000a, 178ff.). But even decoy and deception have changed. Now, in the twenty-first century, with weapons technology having developed beyond first-hand observation, it is also necessary to:

Camouflage *the trajectories*, to direct the enemy's attention away from the true trajectory to lure his surveillance towards false movements, towards illusory trajectories, thanks to decoys, electronic countermeasures that 'seduce' but do not 'requite' their weaponry (Virilio 2002, 54-5; my emphasis).

Scale

Some conflict in the twentieth century has been labelled 'total war'. War in this period typically extended beyond the confines of a discrete battle*field*, first to take in (and ultimately take out) the entire landscape (e.g. the Western Front in World War I), extending to a global scale and incorporating sea-, air- and landscape in World War II, and impacting on everybody, however far from the front-line they may be. This developed into the risk of mutual destruction and the reality of environmental pollution (Kuletz 1998) with the physical limits extending to an infinite degree into space (e.g. with the Star Wars programme) during the Cold War. Again this development and increase in scale is dictated by technological capability, with the desire to win the 'space race' and take a significant lead in the Cold War being driven by military agenda, and itself driving forward Research and Development programmes.

Capability is one thing, but the impact of weapons is quite another, and the threat of global meltdown in the Cold War dominated many people's experience of this period. Again Virilio's progression can be seen, from hand-to-hand combat and warfare at the scale of one's own personal space, to weapons that delivered munitions from a distance and could have more impact in the sense of targeting numbers of troops and the places that contain or protect them, to those devices (now known to all as Weapons of Mass Destruction) which have the potential to be remotely triggered, and could destroy entire regions, with wider global impact. The effects of such weapons are known through testing programmes, for example in the

Pacific and the Nevada Test Site in the United States, and their use at Hiroshima and Nagasaki in 1945.

Alliances

Alliances aren't entirely new, though their influence on the material culture of twentieth-century warfare has been profound. This is especially the case for World War II and the Cold War. It is only through appreciating alliance in World War II, for example, that we can begin to understand why, three years after Britain stood alone in 1940, American troops and aircraft filled the country. Membership of NATO (the North Atlantic Treaty Organisation) as an alliance effectively against Communism explains the presence of United States troops manning cruise missiles on RAF bases in England, and the presence of German 'Panzer' tanks at the Castlemartin ranges in Wales during the Cold War. The infrastructure resulting from the UK's membership of NATO was based on the operational requirements of the Alliance and not necessarily those of Britain. Furthermore, these structures were built to NATO and not necessarily British standards and specifications, points that need to be born in mind when recording and interpreting the buildings and sites that remain (Cocroft 2001; Cocroft and Thomas 2003).

All of this is true also for the Warsaw Pact. In fact some of the most interesting research questions to emerge from the Cold War concern the contrasting experiences of the period among those in each of these two alliances. How different were (conscripted) Russian service personnel's experiences of the Cold War on a base in East Germany, from that of US personnel based at Greenham Common, for example, and how might those differences be recognised through the material record?

1. Characterising combat archaeology

Reporting and representation

A war of pictures and sounds is replacing the war of objects ... In a technician's version of an all-seeing Divinity, ever ruling out accident and surprise, the drive is on for a general system of illumination that will allow everything to be seen and known, at every moment and in every place (Virilio 1984).

Technological developments have enabled a closer proximity to exist between events and their audience. While in World War I and II relatives and friends would watch newsreel accounts, and read the words of war correspondents in newspapers and official reports, they were some distance from the action, and from the reality of a front-line experience. But with recent wars that situation has changed. Journalists are now often 'embedded' within the armed forces, providing first-hand accounts of the action. Some journalists and cameramen have died while on active service. Satellite technology enables the instantaneous communication of their reports, so action is reported in real time, into homes around the world. This proximity introduces a degree of reality to our experience of conflict, a point of particular relevance where death or atrocity is witnessed. Arguably, we are also better informed than we once were, being now virtual participants, albeit some physical distance away from the action. This is true also for service personnel and their families. At the start of the century there was no contact for months and sometimes years between a serviceman away from home and his family; now mobile telephones and welfare calls ensure close and regular contact.

*

What this context provides is a recognition of the type of

warfare that has developed during the twentieth century, its increasing impact on society and landscape, the significance of the reflexive relationship that existed with Research and Development in technological and information technological fields, and the close proximity that can now exist between the theatre of war and its wider audience (in fact with the War on Terror, the theatre now extends to all major cities and beyond). This then is the context within which to critically appraise the material culture of war and conflict during this period. It is only by understanding the importance of speed and technology, for example, that the significance of some of the places that drove warfare to a faster pace can be assessed, and a credible archaeological research framework established to assess that significance and research it more fully. The next section examines what archaeology can contribute to this subject, beyond what we can learn from other sources and disciplines.

Why do we need an archaeology of modern conflict?

There are really two separate questions here: first, does archaeology as an applied discipline have relevance for studying the modern period at all; and second, can archaeology make a significant contribution to something as well documented (e.g. through oral historical sources, archives, official histories) as conflict?

Contemporary archaeology

I should begin by stating that, for me, archaeology isn't a thing (as in, 'what can the archaeology tell us?') but a way of looking at the past. Strictly speaking it is therefore misleading to separate out 'buildings' or 'documents' from 'archaeology', for example, as buildings, documents and buried archaeological remains are equally a part of archaeological study; they are all material evidence that archaeologists are trained to investigate. But on occasion, in the chapters that follow, this distinction between physical and documentary evidence will be made where clarity requires it.

That said, much attention has been paid recently to developing an archaeological methodology for the recent past (by which is generally meant the twentieth century) and within that the contemporary past (that of which we have direct personal experience). Notable among these developments have been collections of related work on the subject of material culture (Graves Brown 2000), its use and interpretation (Buchli and Lucas 2001) and management (e.g. MacDonald 1996; Jones 2002). Previously the emphasis was on studying the present as a means to providing models for interpreting the distant past. Among many others, Gould and Schiffer (1981) noted how ethnoarchaeological studies of modern societies could be used to test assumptions about archaeological evidence, largely among hunter-gatherer groups (this can also be viewed in reverse, a kind of 'archaeoethnography': one colleague noted how sections of my jointly authored essay about the Greenham Common peace camps [Schofield and Anderton 2000] could have been written as it was only by someone with a grounding in Mesolithic archaeology!).

But recent work has given the archaeology of the modern period a value in itself: as Graves Brown (2000) has described it, for placing a critique on modern life, and for understanding our own society, perhaps with a view to improving it for the future. It also serves the purpose of testing assumptions and preconceptions about the world in which we live; making the familiar unfamiliar, as Buchli and Lucas put it (2001). As future chapters will show, we are sometimes a little too willing to receive wisdom, for example from official histories, or from authority in one form or another. Archaeology, and examining modern material culture with an archaeological methodology and mind-set (in other words using the skills we have been taught and have developed as archaeologists, recognising the primacy of material culture for interpreting past events, and the need to be objective, analytical etc., and questioning *everything*) enables us to challenge these often established and accepted views of society. This does not mean that archaeology has any prior claim or intellectual superiority over other disciplines. Far from it. Instead this is one approach among many, but one perhaps more willing than others to accede to E.O. Wilson's call for trans-disciplinarity; for 'consilience' (2001). Archaeologists are used to this. We routinely work closely with those in other disciplines to interpret the past, and can do so equally well and equally effectively for the present.

Modern archaeology also brings other benefits. It can provide the opportunity to give a voice to those silenced in or by society. Archaeology and ethnicity is a significant field of study, while archaeologists will often play a significant role in discussing ownership claims with traditional or indigenous owners. Archaeology in both of these cases is deeply and unavoidably politicised. But there are examples where archaeology is adopted more as a means to record events that might not otherwise feature in future records of the twentieth century. Much investment has been placed on recording the Cold War landscape of the Nevada Test Site in the United States, for example, where nuclear testing was undertaken between 1951 and 1992 (Johnson and Beck 1995; Beck 2002, 66). In all, 928 nuclear tests were conducted here, and the material legacy is well known from archaeological recording programmes undertaken over the past decade. These have had the purpose of providing an historic record of the fabric, to accompany in time the detailed scientific data on each experiment undertaken, and the oral historical evidence of those involved. It is also recognised that a detailed record of these buildings will be needed to

Fig. 1.2. Reflector tower, Area 6 at the Nevada Test Site, USA.

determine future management needs, if some are to be retained, for example (Figure 1.2). But beyond the Test Site is the Peace Camp, occupied for much of the time the Test Site was operational by a diverse community of peace activists. Until 2001 this extensive archaeological site had no record, and was known only through the experiences of those present on the camp, and those responsible for arresting them. For the Peace Camp therefore, archaeological recording was more concerned with providing a balanced interpretation of past events: ensuring that history did not merely recall the test facility, without the material record left by its opponents (Schofield, Beck and Drollinger 2003).

A further justification for archaeology of this modern period concerns its protection and the notion of retaining representative selections of sites for future generations to learn about or draw benefit from. This is true of every period, yet for the modern era we have an advantage. In determining which Roman or prehistoric monuments to preserve, or to record, we are working with an unknown sample of the original population. In England, we know from recent studies how many sites have been lost to agriculture, coast erosion and development over the last fifty years (Darvill and Fulton 1998), yet we are less certain of the original population for each monument class. And we don't know how many classes of monument there were; the more ephemeral, and arguably the more representative of society may have been lost altogether.

For modern sites the primary historical and documentary sources provide that information, so that decisions can be made on the basis of a sound understanding of the whole resource. Most World War II sites, for example, have been lost since 1945 (Anderton and Schofield 1999; Schofield 2002a), yet this fact is at least now documented and can be accommodated in management decision-making. For the Cold War era, the position is stronger still. The period is close (contemporary for many of us) and we have recognised its cultural significance early enough to document what was built and ensure that the selection of sites for retention can be truly representative. For the first time, in other words, decisions are being taken before the 'erosion of history' begins. Examples of the management process and how it relates to recent military heritage are the subject of Chapter 4.

Archaeological treatment of the recent past is astonishingly popular, in part because it directly impacts upon people's lives and memories, and because it taps into a certain curiosity about what archaeology can contribute when we apparently know so much already. Television coverage of archaeology has proliferated in the last decade, with increasing attention paid to recent military and industrial sites in the last four to five years: Channel 4's Time Team has covered World War II crash site excavations in Norfolk and France, and D-Day battlefields; BBC's Meet the Ancestors and related programmes began to explore the connections between archaeology and memory, initially through a 1950s civilian air crash in the Sahara Desert; and Time Flyers have examined through reconstruction the effectiveness of World War II bombing decoys for Hull. The BBC's Restoration featured Harperley World War II prisoner of war camp in its first series, and the Bawdsey radar station in the second. These programmes routinely attract 2.5 to 3.5 million viewers.

This brings us to a final justification for creating an archaeology of the recent and contemporary past and one that takes us back to the significance of personal experience and intimacy referred to earlier: memory. The World War II prisoner of war camp at Harperley (Co. Durham) introduced the unusual situation of an English Heritage inspector being directly involved in the protection and future management of the camp where her father was held prisoner (Nieke and Nieke 2003). This dilemma (as it became) promoted a dialogue about the place, and memories of it, that had not previously occurred. It created a situation whereby photographs could be scrutinised and stories told. It provided the opportunity for memories and motivations to be addressed in the context of wider discussions about the site's future use.

In terms of archaeological practice, studying this modern period is like studying any period: it is concerned with creating a record, interpreting that record and asking questions of it. It is often assumed that with written sources we must know everything. The presence of written sources certainly helps, in that they provide much by way of social, economic and political context for any enquiry. But as is often said, the more we know, the more questions are generated, and it will be those (generally more detailed) questions – often about the sites themselves – that archaeology can address most effectively.

This brings us onto the second question: what archaeology can usefully contribute to a subject apparently so well understood – modern conflict.

Towards an archaeology of modern conflict

As with any archaeological study of the modern period, the techniques and skills available to archaeologists studying modern conflict will generally be similar to those for earlier periods. But there are exceptions (such as the availability of oral historical evidence), and the motivations may be different. Some excavation, for example, may be undertaken specifically for reasons of commemoration or remembrance; to re-establish the memory of a specific event, or a person through the physical act of recovery. This may be the case with some aircraft crash-site excavations, for example (Legendre 2001; Holyoak 2002). It was also true for excavations at Cape Town's District Six, where former residents, removed under the apartheid regime's Group Areas Act, began to re-establish a degree of ownership (Malan

and Soudien 2002) through excavation and artistic intervention. In some cases excavation will be conducted to recover
human remains lost in battle, for internment on home soil (such
as the USA's Missing in Action teams, cf. Hoshower-Leppo
2002), or for reasons of justice and retribution (Saunders, R.
2002). But otherwise the motivations for archaeological work
can apply to sites of any type or period: some work provides
information as the basis for monument management
schemes (e.g. Cave 2000); some will be purely for interpretation and furtherance of knowledge; and some to create the
historic record in advance of development or to satisfy planning conditions.

Sources are worth outlining here, although examples later in
the book will provide more detail on each. The role of documentary sources in providing contextual information on the
archaeology of modern conflict is now well known and generally
accepted. Between 1995 and 2001 English Heritage commissioned a study (the Twentieth Century Fortifications in
England Project) that generated reports on eleven of the major
classes of military archaeological sites (Dobinson et al. 1997 for
a summary; Dobinson 2000a; 2001 for published examples).
This project used primary sources held at the Public Record
Office (now the National Archives) to establish information on
location, typology and the strategic context for construction for,
among other classes: coast artillery; anti-aircraft artillery;
bombing decoys; radar; and civil defence sites. For most of these
classes of monument the project revealed where all the sites
were and when, and what they looked like (Dobinson et al.
1997), providing a 'manual' for investigators in the field. More
of this project is described in Chapters 2 and 3.

One of the main problems with primary sources of this type
is their accessibility – their availability for public scrutiny.
Freedom of information in the United States means that at
least some documents are generally available on most things,

even for the later years of the Cold War and such sensitive topics as the nuclear testing programme. But in the UK what is commonly referred to as the Thirty Year Rule means that documents will be selectively released only once thirty years have elapsed, and for some of the more sensitive material this may be considerably longer (though in the UK, a new Freedom of Information Act [2005] is likely to have implications for future study). This longer delay will occur where files contain distressing personal information about people and events, or where information might damage national security or international relations, or where it was supplied subject to confidential undertakings. This is referred to as 'extended closure' and may be for 50, 75 or 100 years (for more information see www.pro.gov.uk/about/access). But this is both a problem (in that some documents aren't available for study), and an opportunity, to which I will return shortly.

Additional to the Thirty Year Rule in the UK is the Official Secrets Act 1989, to which Crown servants are subject. Under this Act, it is an offence to disclose official information in six categories without lawful authority and if the disclosure is damaging to the national interest. The six categories are:

Security and intelligence
Defence
International relations
Foreign confidences
Information that might lead to the commission of a crime
Special investigation powers under the Interception of Communications Act 1985 and the Security Services Act 1989.

The Official Secrets Act is a document that cannot be 'unsigned'. And this is where the opportunity comes in. For sites where documents remain closed, and former employees remain bound (or believe they remain bound) by the Official Secrets

1. Characterising combat archaeology

Act, archaeology, and the analytical and interpretative skills of archaeologists, are the only methods of interpretation available, and this may remain the case for our lifetime. In some cases local planning authorities or national heritage agencies will have to understand a site sufficiently to determine significance and/or future management needs. Where documents and oral historical evidence are not available, archaeology – and generally in this context that means archaeological survey – provides a viable alternative. This is in part what happened at Spadeadam (Cumbria), though here former rocket scientists were also involved in interpreting remains of the Blue Streak testing facilities (Tuck et al. 2004; Wilson 2003, in press).

One concern sometimes expressed is that documents may provide evidence for what was intended, and not necessarily what was built. In fact this is a question more of the skills needed to interpret documents and being aware of the possibilities that sites were not completed, rather than being an inherent difficulty with the source itself.

This doesn't however mean that field archaeology is redundant where documents and oral historical evidence are available. Rather these are the very sites where the various sources of information can be critically appraised. The sources may serve to confirm each other's validity, perhaps with oral historical evidence adding details or 'colour' to the rather dry functional interpretation provided by historical sources. Or there may be discrepancies. Take the case of the World War II bombing decoy at Blackdown, Somerset (Schofield et al. 2001). Here field remains and oral historical evidence were compared with documentary records to build an interpretation, one that involved balancing and assessing inconsistencies in the evidence. Most significant here was the fact that personal accounts perpetuated the wartime myth of mounds on Blackdown representing the decoy town, whereas in fact they represented

37

anti-landing obstacles; the decoys (of which there were several) were separate (ibid., 284) and their physical remains far more ephemeral. Yet with the decoys we wouldn't have known either what we were looking for or precisely where to look if it had not been for documentary sources (cited in Dobinson 2000a).

Archaeologists studying modern warfare need to be aware of the benefits and pitfalls of the sources at their disposal. It is also helpful to develop a methodology that draws upon all of these sources to provide the information that they are best placed to deliver. Documentary sources can provide the national and strategic context for sites; they can provide detailed accounts of construction and supply, and a site's military record in terms of engagement or its wider strategic role. Documents can also be used to interpret the implementation of government policy and strategic decisions on a local scale. The various changes of approach to anti-invasion defence in the UK in 1940-1, for example, can be read in cabinet papers, while implementation can be seen at local level in the War Diaries and ultimately in each area's Defence Scheme, being a detailed record of what was built, where and why (Dobinson 1996a, Foot 2004). These schemes also describe who would be responsible for manning each area and position, and with what weapons.

Oral historical evidence tells how it was for those involved. The passage of time and failing memory can be factors in interpreting these first-hand accounts, yet they will nevertheless reflect reality and create often highly emotive and engaging narratives about sites that might otherwise be historic, or even effectively 'prehistoric' where the documents remain – for now – unavailable. The Heritage Lottery Fund is currently putting D-Day veterans in contact with local schools to promote awareness and encourage the use of oral history as a significant resource for understanding the recent past.

1. Characterising combat archaeology

The Cold War as prehistory

It is a paradox that the recent past, and the period often within living memory, can be deemed characteristically modern, historic or prehistoric depending on how we as archaeologists can approach the field remains. Sites can be approached as being truly modern where we can draw on oral historical evidence and available primary sources (generally over thirty years ago for the primary sources, and up to, say, sixty years ago for oral historical accounts), historic where material remains ('archaeology' in the conventional sense) combine only with documents (for sites generally over sixty years old), and prehistoric where only the archaeological evidence is available (say less than thirty years ago, as many employed at these sites – and certainly those whose particular roles will help interpretation – may consider themselves bound by the Official Secrets Act). Table 1.2 takes another look at the various ages of war.

Dates/Examples	Age	Evidence
1974-2004 [e.g. Cold War; post Cold War]	'Prehistoric'	archaeological evidence no access to oral histories (Official Secrets Act) no access to documents (30 Yrs Rule)
1934-1974 [e.g. World War II; early Cold War]	'Modern'	archaeological evidence oral history primary sources
1900-1934 [e.g. Boer War and World War I]	'Historic'	archaeological evidence no oral histories (except those previously recorded) primary sources

Table 1.2. The ages of war (2).

But, as before, it is more complicated than that. Some classes of site are more likely to instil a degree of secrecy among former

employees than others, while some military research programmes or operations may remain classified for longer, given
sensitivities and perceived public reaction. Either way, the
skills required to study the archaeology of modern conflict will
need to take the details of this paradox into account, just as they
will the nature of the material record. It is also true that the
boundaries will constantly shift towards the present, as oral
historical evidence ceases to be available for earlier periods and
as documents are released.

2

The matériel culture of modern conflict

Barbed wire

In Olivier Razac's book *Barbed Wire: a political history* (2002, 3), he describes barbed wire as being 'everywhere, and since its invention used throughout the world, in all kinds of ways and with different objectives, even contradictory ones. For these reasons, its history seems too chaotic to chart.' Nevertheless this is what he attempts, describing its role in agriculture, demarcation and division, and war. Its attributes and significance predominate throughout, illustrating the role of material culture in society and for constructing memory.

Barbed wire was a salient attribute of the memory of the Great War. It never became a metaphor for the war, because it does not symbolise the entire conflict, or even the fighting in the trenches. Nevertheless, barbed wire could be said to have the 'artistic' role of evoking the monstrous sublimity of the forces of destruction liberated by modern war. In the account and images of the Great War, barbed wire is significant only as a part of an overall aesthetic. Only after the war did it become a universal symbol of the whole. Its decisive role in the Nazi concentration and extermination camps made barbed wire the symbol of the worst catastrophe of the century (ibid., 52).

41

We shall return to barbed wire later in the chapter.

Material cultures

This chapter will describe the scope and diverse range of material culture that represents modern conflict. In some longer-term histories of warfare strong distinctions were drawn between the various materials used to wage war and support combatants in the field, each reflecting a period in which their significance was predominant; for example, stone, flesh, iron and fire (Keegan 1993). This chapter will follow that model to a degree, presenting material culture according to the nature of the evidence, while recognising that this approach has limitations and is adopted entirely for convenience and clarity. Other equally valid frameworks for presenting this material culture include those based upon: speed and technological development (e.g. Virilio and Lotringer 1997); ideology and opposition (e.g. East and West; bunkers and benders); and the 'teeth' and 'tail' of the armed forces, being partly the distinction between social and military archaeology, and partly that between operations and logistics. Later chapters – and specifically those that describe presenting and interpreting the archaeology of modern warfare, and management – will draw this evidence together into a more coherent and unified archaeology than is attempted here.

This chapter therefore presents modern military archaeology in the following terms:

Landscape – in the sense of impacts upon the landscape and influences over it
Buildings
Monuments (i.e. places that no longer have a use as buildings; places that have gone out of use)
Memorials

2. The matériel culture of modern conflict

Vehicles, vessels and aircraft
Artefacts
Voices (oral historical evidence)
Words (written sources)
Photographs and film
Artistic expression

The purpose here is to provide a brief critical outline of each of these categories, with examples and suggested further reading. A short summary and overview will draw these strands together at the close of the chapter.

Landscape

Landscape has had many definitions, not all of them particularly helpful. But the recent definition provided by the European Landscape Convention (in Fairclough and Rippon 2002, 228) seems to fit most closely with the types of material culture, perceptual frameworks and experiences described in this book. It describes landscape as meaning:

> an area, as perceived by people, whose character is the result of the action and interaction of natural and/or human factors.

As Fairclough has explained, this definition is underpinned by two powerful and inter-related ideas: First, that landscape belongs to everyday life, as part of every citizen's culture, heritage and environment, and must be democratised both in terms of identifying why it is valuable and deciding how it is used. Second, that landscape is a cultural construct composed of many different ways of understanding and appreciation, not all of which are scientific, objective or material; many are personal, individual and subjective, or reflect intangible aspects of the environment. It is recognised that both ideas present challenges to archaeologists (Fairclough 2002, 25).

The militarised landscape sits comfortably within this wider definition. It includes the deliberate creation or manipulation of landscape, for the purposes of military use and occupation. It also includes what is sometimes referred to as relict cultural landscape, being those places that either retain traces of their military historic past (e.g. battlefields), or where the presence of military units has both preserved earlier cultural and natural heritage, as well as adding new layers in the form of military archaeological remains. It also includes those areas that have been and in some cases continue to be influenced by the presence of military units or personnel, such as the 'bomber landscapes' of Lincolnshire in World War II, where the transient population of air force personnel (British, Americans and other allies) impacted upon rural social networks. Landscape also extends beyond terrestrial regions to include landscapes in the air and at sea: the battlefields of the Battle of Britain (air) and the Battle of the Atlantic (sea), for example, both of which have been the subject of consideration, including as cultural landscapes (Parham pers comm. for Battle of the Atlantic; Lake and Schofield 2000 for Battle of Britain). Recent studies of the Cold War have extended this definition still further to include space: the geographically and theoretically infinite spheres formally defined by Star Wars and related Cold War and post Cold War defence policy (Gorman 2005), though recognising that space had earlier relevance through use of the ionosphere for long distance wireless, and later for surveillance and communications.

Landscape is the broadest scale at which the influence of military activity can be felt and assessed. It is also the scale at which the impact of conflict can be best appreciated, whether upon the form of the physical landscape, or on the psychology of its inhabitants. An example of physical impact is the influence of the Front Line on the landscape of northern France and Belgium. Here five years of conflict created a scarred, levelled and empty land, with its settlements (like Ypres) reduced to rubble, and the subsistence base ruined. Even now, nearly ninety years later, the deadly legacy of this battle remains, and unexploded ordnance creates new victims every year. But the impact remains in other ways too. It is a landscape of commemoration, with cemeteries scattered over the region, the inscriptions and dates on the gravestones and in the record books that accompany every cemetery telling the story of the conflict and of its victims. Some of the battlefields are also now sacred sites, some being presented specifically as places of memory. The battlefield sites at Vimy Ridge and Beaumont Hamel, for example, managed by Veterans Affairs Canada, are both memorials and also archaeological sites: the trench systems, shell holes, tunnels and other landmarks all remain. The landscape is also now a museum landscape, with numerous larger (at Flanders Fields in Ypres) and smaller (roadside and café) museums to feed the burgeoning interest that now exists for World War I battlefield tourism. Finally it remains a living and working landscape, albeit with all the hazards of a former battle to contend with. Nicholas Saunders describes the area as a:

> multi-vocal landscape: an industrialised slaughter house, a vast tomb for 'The Missing', a landscape of memorialisation and pilgrimage, a location for archaeological investigation, cultural heritage development and tourism (2002a, 106).

There are two ways of interpreting this landscape. We can consider it as a landscape in which a battle occurred, and view it from the perspective of historical overview, as a map, a landscape extending the length of the Front with a significant zone of influence in front of and behind it. We can also take the

Fig. 2.1. A moment from Lucy Orta's installation *Transgressing Fashion, #0204*, timed to coincide with the handover of Iraq, June 2004.

soldier's perspective, and view it in experiential terms, as specific places within the wider battlefield, and more in terms of viewsheds, fields of fire, concealment, positions, obstacles and protection. This is still landscape, but at the scale at which combatants themselves would have understood and experienced the battle. I recently participated in an installation by the artist Lucy Orta. *Transgressing Fashion* involved fifty models wearing combat suits and gas masks, decorated with silver and gold leaf, walking in a long line through galleries at the V&A Museum, London, and standing in choreographed positions, in rows and grids. The similarities with a soldier's experience in battle struck me: in this situation one has a very limited view, and relies upon/is influenced by and engages with only close neighbours. The wider scene can only be viewed and experienced by others, looking on (Figure 2.1).

2. The matériel culture of modern conflict

Landscape is also useful for assessing the degree to which places become militarised or industrial (and these two things are often closely related). Here are two examples. First, in February 1944 in the UK some 11.5 million acres were under military control for military purposes. This represented some 20% of the total land area of Britain (Foot 1998). Included within this figure were some 740 airfields of various types (bomber and fighter airfields, for example, satellite landing grounds and dispersals), hundreds and perhaps up to a thousand army camps, large numbers of requisitioned buildings, prisoner of war camps (Thomas 2003) and hundreds of military training areas (Dobinson 2000b), for Army, Royal Naval and Royal Air Force personnel. In 1940-1 the invasion threat was at its height, and defence policy reflected that fact. As a result first one strategy (defensive 'stop'-lines) and then another (area defence) were adopted and implemented, with defensive positions constructed across Britain, and especially in those areas more likely to be enemy targets (e.g. industrial centres, cities, transport and infrastructure). Anti-tank ditches were constructed, and pillboxes (probably over 20,000) were built, all designed to create defended landscapes. Each area was described in a Defence Scheme, a detailed manual of what had to be built and where, and how the area should be defended. The entire country was covered by one Defence Scheme or another. And beyond these closely defined landscapes were other militarised places such as anti-aircraft batteries, bombing decoys (to deceive enemy bomb aimers into hitting dummy targets instead of the real ones), barrage balloon sites, searchlights and so on. The entire country was a landscape at war. As Churchill said in August 1940, 'the fronts are everywhere. The trenches are dug in the towns and streets. Every village is fortified. Every road is barred. The whole British Army is at home .... The whole Island bristles against invaders, from the sea or from the air ... .'

The second example demonstrates the strong connections that exist between militarised and industrial landscapes, and the sheer scale of the influence of militarisation, spatially and socially. A good way to begin to understand the impact of Valerie Kuletz's *Tainted Desert* (1998), is to start with the lists of maps and illustrations, the symbols used on those maps, and the acronyms. In all, the book contains twenty-nine maps showing, for example, areas she collectively describes as the 'nuclear landscape', activists' maps of these areas showing places with higher than normal plutonium readings, nuclear waste shipment routes, radioactive waste dumps and military land withdrawals and controlled air space. Symbols include those for National Laboratories, sites for nuclear waste burial, military reservations, uranium production sites and so on. The acronyms divide into those which are governmental (e.g. Los Alamos National Laboratory) and non-governmental (e.g. Native Americans for a Clean Environment).

The 'landscape' of this book is the American Midwest, and the theme is environmental and social ruin. Its author is the daughter of a weapons scientist, again emphasising the curious connections that sometimes exist in studies of the recent past. As Kuletz states (1998, 5), the American Midwest is a nuclear landscape, 'too often ripened by sacrifice, for sacrifice, shrouded in secrecy, and plundered of its wealth'. Science and the military have transformed this landscape. Within it,

> stand thousands of abandoned and unreclaimed open-pit and underground uranium mines and mills, two proposed national sites for deep geologic nuclear waste repositories of monumental proportions, all potential sites for the nation's above-ground temporary nuclear waste containment facilities, a constellation of other nuclear pollution points ... and secret testing sites. ... This region contains important nuclear research and development centers,

with their own 'private' on-site nuclear waste disposal
areas of significant size. The region has seen more military land withdrawals than any other region in the United
States, eliminating many millions of acres of land from
public access, transforming whole mountain ranges into
massive nuclear weapons testing theatres. Finally it contains a site where shallow burial or 'low-level' nuclear
waste is scheduled to occur (Kuletz 1997, 10-11).

But as well as being a technological landscape, heavily developed for military purposes, it is also a sacred Indian landscape,
a place where 'spiritual and cultural life are woven directly into
the landscape itself' (ibid., 13). Many consider it a wasteland, a
landscape of national sacrifice; an expendable landscape. It is a
landscape loaded with symbols of power exerted by the military
over the land and its former and current occupants: high fences,
watch-towers, radar antennae and signs; roads to nowhere;
sonic booms and occasional glimpses of a Stealth aircraft complete the experience. The region also maintains what Kuletz
calls 'Science Cities', places that have developed primarily on
government funded projects and defence money. Some were
started from scratch, while others were urban areas resusci-
tated by government money, intellectuals and the growth of
infrastructure and services to support its primary purpose.
Kuletz identifies zones within the nuclear landscape; places
where militarisation is focused and concentrated. Her Zone
One, in northern New Mexico, takes in the Los Alamos National
Laboratory. She describes this zone as

a layer of nuclearism and militarization superimposed
upon a landscape that has been historically imprinted
with more Indian and Hispanic presence than any other
region in the United States. To the uranium mining fields
can now be added the 43-square-mile-campus of Los

Alamos, Sandia Labs with its massive weapons arsenal, Kirkland Air Force Base ... and the 4000 square miles of desert that is White Sands Missile Range, with the Fort Bliss Military Reservation, as well as other military reserves, extending the militarised zone all the way into Texas. Because of the nature of radiation and toxic chemicals, all these installations reach far beyond their borders of influence (ibid., 59).

These landscapes can be described and perceived in different ways. But from an archaeological perspective the significance of this example is partly its scale and zone of influence (i.e. there is a military-*related* landscape and a military-*affected* landscape, and these will differ in extent depending on whether our focus is primarily material culture, or extending to its wider public health implications). It is also significant in the diversity of components that contribute to this landscape of power. However, referring to the definition of landscape contained within the European Landscape Convention, it is not merely the tangible remnants that give this place relevance for archaeological study. It is also about the character of the region, and the interrelationships between the various layers of significance that coexist here. It is about the community, in other words, and their perceptions of risk, beauty, interference and the continued occupation and use by military personnel. All of these things should matter to us, and form part of any archaeological enquiry.

Finally, at landscape scale is the presence of militarised boundaries or barriers and their impact. Visually boundaries are strong on meaning and symbolism; they are typically controlling and influential and are most tangible at crossing points and frontiers (Dolff-Bonekaemper 2004). What interests us here though is their impact at landscape-scale, whether actual or perceived. One example of a boundary that was imposed and then removed as suddenly as it arrived was the Iron Curtain that separated East from West over a period of thirty to forty years. Best known of its component parts is the Berlin Wall (Baker 1993, Feversham and Schmidt 2001; Dolff-Bonekaemper 2002; Klausmeier and Schmidt 2004; Schmidt and von Preuschen 2005), though the Iron Curtain itself to the west of Berlin was larger, deeper and its impact at landscape scale arguably easier to see. Szpenowski (2002), for example, describes changes following the fall of the Iron Curtain in 1989. He records the decline of intensive agriculture, the legacy of the state farms which collapsed simultaneously with the Communist and Socialist systems, and the rise of new farming strategies, and how these new strategies are providing opportunities for the sustained protection of the cultural landscape. These are changes that can be read in the modern landscape; part of the longer-term processes of change and continuity that archaeology is well-placed to study.

Buildings

Some of the most tangible traces of former military activity are the many buildings that remain in use, or were once used for military purposes. These can range from domestic buildings such as barrack, mess or housing stock (e.g. married quarters), to specialised buildings like control towers and hangars, workshops and factories. Where they remain comparatively complete and maintain their original appearance and form, these buildings give a sense of authenticity to visitors, combined in most cases with some sense of history, as for example with a World War II control tower. They give an indication of the conditions under which people lived and operated; they will often provide an interpretive framework for the activities known to have been conducted within the building; and they enable former occupants and employees to maintain a sense of belonging to and ownership of the past.

Barrack buildings are an example of the way military architecture has been examined in recent years more according to its role in society (Douet 1998), than as a building type per se. Douet's study reviewed how the planning and architecture of barracks in the period 1600-1914 were effected by

> the structure of human relationships and the patterns of social behaviour within the armed forces. After all, the erection and planning of the buildings was intended to facilitate the effective working of the military organism. The military routine of drill and training, and the daily rhythm of eating, washing and sleeping were obviously overriding influences, but they were overlain by concepts of the integrity of the unit, of the relationship between the officers and the other ranks, and between the military and civilian worlds (Douet 1998, xiv).

Douet cites the regularity of layout and plan-form and the parade ground as examples of significant components of barracks, but also recognising closure and separation as holding significance in terms of design and guiding principles. Barrack plans sought to exclude the outside civilian world, for example. As Douet has described, 'the harmful effects of lax or hostile civilian life on discipline, loyalty and security were in part what prompted States to provide specialised quarters in the first place' (ibid., xvi). The basic and recurring themes in barrack design include this closure and separation. Another characteristic is the formal regularity of site plan, with soldiers' blocks arranged symmetrically around the communal space of the parade ground or square. This was the significant and central ceremonial space, for assembly of troops, drill and parades. It was also used for instruction and was the scene of disciplinary action. It was overlooked by the principal accommodation buildings constructed along its sides, and was central to the design in all senses (ibid.).

Changes of circumstance, both in the military and within society in general, can allow flexibility in apparently rigid design principles. As Douet has noted, the concept of symmetrical inward-looking central parade grounds was maintained until the middle of the nineteenth century. After that a more varied typology developed, in which declining hostility reduced the need for barracks to be built for maintaining civil order, coincident with an increase in the complexity of military society, as sergeants and other non-commissioned officers acquired their own messes and quarters.

Buildings that remain in their original form, or where plan-form survives sufficiently to enable a full interpretation of layout, have added value in understanding patterns of use. This can be applied to the industrial production process, interpreting a factory or military-industrial building in terms of the flow of material and production within it, from the arrival of raw material to the removal of munitions, for example. Techniques have also been developed for examining social space within buildings of various types (e.g. Foster 1989; Gould 1995), and these can have application in terms of studying, for example, mess buildings, using this 'access analysis' to examine the way space is controlled and demarcated by convention, order and discipline, to investigate the degree to which the buildings reflect social structure and social relations. A comparable approach has recently been taken to recording and interpreting buildings at Bletchley Park, used for codebreaking during World War II. Here the allocation of space, and flow of information between and through buildings has been modelled, based both on the physical structures that remain and oral historical evidence. It is known, for example, that a vacuum tube system was developed for passing information between huts; there were also conveyor belts, and steel tubes were built under the roads to connect the huts. There are many instances here where developments in Signals and Intelligence (SIGINT) can be related directly to fabric and to the buildings that survive. A detailed record of these is now available following a study by English Heritage (English Heritage 2004b).

Another approach has been to examine military sites and buildings within the context of anthropologically-derived theories, for example concerning the use of control over movements of personnel. An example cited by Anderton (2002) is the tendency for the guardroom and officers' quarters to be close to the entrance of World War II coast batteries, while soldiers' quarters were further into the site, closer to its operational centre. Two considerations are relevant here, and combine to determine this aspect of layout: on the one hand the entirely pragmatic consideration of placing those responsible for manning the guns close to the guns. But another less obvious consideration concerns social control. As Anderton puts it, by entering the site and passing the officers' quarters, 'the soldiers' journey through social narrative was obvious, a point reinforced with images of the contemporary hierarchical status through the prominent location of the officers' quarters' (2002, 192).

Military buildings present two further challenges. First, in terms of conservation, many buildings were not built to last. They were constructed quickly, and often from poor materials (Figure 2.2). Some were timber; others were of corrugated sheeting on a concrete base, while others still were of brick or concrete, but hurriedly constructed. Much of the building work was contracted out, so that some at least was undertaken by reputable construction firms, many of which are major property developers today. Nevertheless, what survives is often unstable and vulnerable to continuing processes of erosion and decay.

Second is that, while recognising the vulnerability of this resource, and significant losses suffered over the past hundred

Fig. 2.2. Wartime buildings, typically designed not to last.

years or so, it is also important to acknowledge the diversity of building types, and the often quite subtle variations in design, reflective of technological change and social conditions, as we saw earlier with barracks. An example of the sheer diversity of types can be found in *British Military Airfield Architecture* (Francis 1996). The chapter on hangars, for example, demonstrates the degree of variation, the terms under which a typology can be established from documentary sources, and how that diversity can then be translated into field observations, and the interpretation of individual sites. The same is true of control towers, of which many types exist, their form and emerging sophistication a reflection of, among other things, developments in radio communications technology. The interpretation of space within these control towers can be viewed in terms of gathering and using information, controlling air movements and observation. These control towers also have value for sense of place; this is where the 'ghosts of place' are often first encountered (Bell 1997). It was from here that aircraft were counted out and counted back, and where people gathered to await their return. It is often these buildings to which veterans first return on revisiting their former stations (Schofield 2002b).

Monuments

Field monuments are taken to mean those places that have fallen out of use and survive as ruined buildings or earthwork constructions; some will now be buried, surviving in a truly archaeological context, hidden from view. For some only a fragmented buried component will survive. As with monuments of earlier periods, we can classify these recent military monuments according to categories, classes and types: the categories are grouped thematically, while the classes are distinctive and specific, and generally subdivide into types, in the same way as bowl, bell, saucer and disc are all classes of Bronze Age round barrow, each then dividing into types, some of which are regionally distinctive. A typology has been established for military sites, and exists in the various volumes resulting from the Twentieth Century Fortifications in England project (e.g. Dobinson 1996a), in the Defence of Britain Project report (www.britarch.ac.uk/projects.dob/review/index.html), and summarised in the recently published Modern Military Matters research framework (Schofield 2004). A classification for Cold War sites appears in Chapter 4. These monuments have value in their own terms, as historic places that evoke a sense of past and of place and memory, and it is principally for this reason that a selection of such monuments in England have been afforded statutory protection, as scheduled monuments. This too will be discussed further in Chapter 4.

The pillbox is the monument class most commonly associated with Britain's defence heritage, probably because it is the most common of surviving structures, the most widespread and perhaps one of the most enigmatic. It is also the place where

2. The matériel culture of modern conflict

'playful warring' most often takes place (Virilio 1976, 15) after these sites originally fall out of use, giving them pertinence to the many that have used them for recreation at one time or another. Being common and widespread they also have significance in terms of local identity with the recent past. Local communities often 'adopt' their local defence structures (and generally these are pillboxes), and can react angrily when they are proposed for demolition. Pillboxes were effectively infantry positions designed to contribute to the defence either of stoplines or vulnerable positions. There were many types (see Dobinson 1996a; Lowry et al. 1995), the diversity a function of the precise purpose for which they were intended, reflecting differences in the numbers of troops and the types of weapons they housed, the range of locations they were intended to defend, and regional variations in the availability of building supplies. Variations can also be seen in design, some of the private companies commissioned to build pillboxes introducing local design variations.

The recently completed Defence of Britain Project was for the most part a review of these anti-invasion defences (Council for British Archaeology 2002). In all 14,000 anti-invasion defences were recorded, 3,155 in good condition. Some 8,000 of these defences were pillboxes, falling into about ten different types. Some are common: the Type 24 pillbox, for example, of which 1,800 examples were recorded; and some less so, such as the Type 25 pillbox (forty-six examples) and the Norcon (twenty-five). This national survey also provided information about the current use of these monuments. They are too small to have any conventional uses, although recently planning applications have been submitted to convert examples to public conveniences and a restaurant. Many are now used as bat roosts. One has been the scene of a murder, while examples near Colchester were used by roads protesters in their campaign against road widening.

But as with many monuments, their meaning is only truly revealed by landscape scale studies, looking at their distribution and placement with relation to the physical landscape and as a logical system of defence. In England two projects have attempted to contextualise these monuments: the English Heritage Defence Areas project (Foot 2003, 2004); and Lacey's (2003) application of Geographical Information Systems (GIS) to pillbox distribution and placement along the Taunton stop-line.

Foot's (2004) Defence Areas study was commissioned by English Heritage in order to help promote public appreciation of World War II defences at landscape scale, and to provide a basis for taking management decisions. The project took as its basis the Defence of Britain Project data and analysed these data in terms of the cohesion of landscape which both contains much of the defence provision put in place originally, and survives largely unaltered from that which was defended in 1940-1. The intention was therefore to identify those places where the wartime landscape was sufficiently legible in the terms in which it was created to allow interpretation by visitors and researchers. At Waverley Abbey (Surrey), for example, defence structures remain in a landscape setting virtually unchanged over the past sixty years. And this is a landscape that can be given clear meaning through interpretation. The local topography and notably the Farnham Gap, which held strategic significance also in the late Prehistoric and Roman periods, would have acted as the conduit for any invading force en route from the south coast to London, and here the combination of river, settlement and carefully placed defences would have provided the trap, the killing field, adjacent to the ruins of a Cistercian Abbey. Notice boards, a leaflet and the nearby Farnham Museum could all have relevance for interpreting this defence area in an informative and imaginative way.

Along the Taunton stop-line, one of the many defensive

2. *The matériel culture of modern conflict*

stop-lines put in place under the command of General Ironside in 1940 (Dobinson 1996a; Alexander 1998), some 233 pillboxes were planned, alongside gun emplacements, road blocks, railway blocks and demolitions (e.g. of bridges). An associated anti-tank obstacle included some twenty-four miles of waterways, eleven miles of anti-tank ditch and eight miles of artificial obstacles (cited in Lacey 2003, 101). Numerous records have been made of these sites along the Taunton stop-line, though few attempts have attempted to give it context, and understand its spatial configuration and meaning (but note David Hunt's current research, unpublished). By sampling a section of the line, Lacey has attempted this by using GIS to take understanding beyond the monument distribution to explore placement, deployment and strategy in a landscape context. His innovative study involved defining viewsheds (the visual range from each position – mostly pillboxes) and 'firesheds' (their fields of fire) in relation to enemy troops on the ground and in the air to demonstrate the logic of placement and predict success (Figure 2.3). The study has progressed the field of military archaeological studies from the theoretical and the documented on the one hand, and the detailed architectural study of structures on the other, to examining monuments in their landscape setting and their capabilities given the artillery available for use, the real stuff of conventional archaeological field practice. And it has worked. Lacey noted how this technique allowed the relative strength of fortifications to be assessed and evaluated, how the primary role of individual structures could be determined in relation to their fields of fire – their 'firesheds', and how reverse engineering can be used to predict the location or orientation of structures that were subsequently removed.

The popular cultural perceptions of World War II tend to focus on several related events and their associated monument types. Notable among these are the airfields representing the

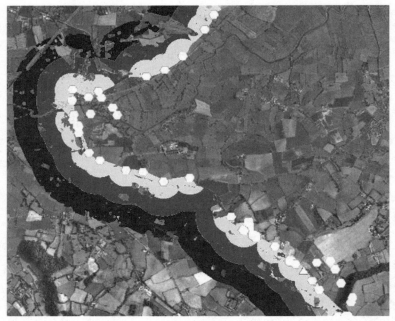

Fig. 2.3. Firesheds from pillboxes (hexagons) and anti-tank guns (triangles) on the Taunton stop-line (after Lacey 2003). Zones to the left (west) of the defences forming the stop-line represent fireshed and viewshed distance boundaries: white – 300 yards (the range for Boys anti-tank rifles); grey – 600 yards (Bren light machine gun); black – 1000 yards (extent of viewshed and maximum range for light machine guns).

Battle of Britain, and the bomber offensive, air-raid shelters, public and private, searchlights, and bomb sites indicative of destruction and fire, and loss of property, family and friends. Less obvious at the time were radar stations whose role was to track enemy bombers and guide our own aircraft towards them; barrage balloons and anti-aircraft sites for the defence of cities; and the bombing decoys designed to fool enemy bomb aimers into hitting dummy targets in place of the real thing (Dobinson 2000a). Together these are the most tangible items, the things which have significance now as monuments of war. Although comparatively rare now, significant numbers of these monuments survive to represent much of this cultural experience, and provide a resource for understanding, appreciation and remembrance.

War cemeteries and memorials

War cemeteries and memorials serve a very particular purpose. These are the places where the war dead are either buried or commemorated, or both, while in some cases they record the scenes of major events. In the immediate aftermath of any conflict, memorials and cemeteries become the focus of commemorative activity, both culturally – in which the act of burial and the associated ceremony provide the context of emotional engagement with loss and the bereaved – and socially for the friends and relatives of the deceased, for whom the burial place and/or memorial gives physical expression to their loss, and a place at which remembering can occur. These places therefore have significant cultural and social value.

A national study of war memorials – the UK National Inventory of War Memorials – was established in 1989 and records details of memorials throughout the UK. In all, 47,000 records have been created, describing memorials that commemorate the Boer Wars, World Wars I and II and the Korean War, for example (Furlong et al. 2002). The study demonstrates how memorial styles have changed and how they reflect both changing attitudes towards those who served in the armed forces in the late nineteenth and twentieth centuries, and regional variations in style and form (e.g. Celtic crosses being most common in Cornwall). It describes the significance of where memorials are positioned in relation to public space, and the increase in secularisation over time with an increasing trend towards memorials on roadsides and village greens (ibid., 17). It also outlines the geographical distribution of memorials; and issues relating to urban and rural memorialisation. It describes the evolution of memorials from being a focus for grief to manifesting veterans' groups' assertions of identity. The physical movement of memorials is also reviewed, ranging from those which have been lost or neglected to include those moved in order to ensure preservation, and the continuation of remembrance services. A significant recent development has been the decision to commemorate those shot for cowardice in World War I – the Shot at Dawn memorial in Staffordshire is an example, funded partly by readers of the *Daily Telegraph* and containing 306 posts, each representing one of those executed. The Private represented here was the son of a gardener, explaining the location in an arboretum and in an area that gets first light at dawn (Black 2004, 144-7).

As numerous authors have suggested, memorials form a significant component in interpreting the scale and impact of conflict on society, and as such constitute an important part of the cultural landscape and its archaeological record (Winter 1995). By travelling through northern France and Belgium, for example, there is now no more eloquent a statement of the scale and impact of World War I than the frequency of war cemeteries; and by visiting just a small selection, and one or two of the memorials, such as the Menin Gate, the full scale of loss can begin to be appreciated. Cemeteries and memorials also have a bearing on how we interpret human responses to conflict. As Tarlow has written:

> The form and location of the memorial not only reflected the grief of the bereaved, but also shaped the expression and understanding of bereavement in war by establishing spatial and figurative structures of remembering. In later years, the emotional force of the memorial was drawn upon and reworked towards the production of other emotional responses. Older, powerful meanings in the

2. *The matériel culture of modern conflict*

memorial – redemption, community, death – were employed in the creation of new meanings – nationalism,
conservatism, religion (1997, 119).

The way in which emotions and rhetoric are granted physical
shape and tangible form is an important area of study. Memorials effectively constitute primary as well as secondary evidence of how nations react to large-scale losses and the way in
which they choose to commemorate their casualties: primary in
terms of a literal recording of how many died; secondary in
terms of people's reaction to that loss and how they chose
memorials which best reflected their feelings. When memorials
were erected, it was broadly considered that they would be cared
for indefinitely and act as a reminder to future generations of the
cost of war, but their evolution shows how people's attitudes and
priorities have changed (Furlong et al. 2002, 34-5).

Vehicles, vessels and aircraft

Collections of objects, frequently privately formed and at personal expense, are often considered to sit rather uneasily on the
fringes of credible conservation efforts, yet these objects –
crashed and perhaps later restored aircraft and their component parts, vessels and military vehicles – are often the very
things that inspire childhood interest, and give meaning and a
sense of authenticity to the often now rather ephemeral and
fragmented places of conflict. Examples include the historic
aircraft that fly from the Imperial War Museum, Duxford
(Cambridgeshire), and military vehicle displays at various military sites and former bases. Historic ships can be visited on the
River Thames (HMS Belfast), at Portsmouth Dockyard and
Chatham, while sunken vessels of World War II are now visited
by over 3,000 divers a year at Chuuk in Micronesia (Jeffery
2004, 52).

But these examples of wartime matériel, I would argue, have value and significance also as archaeological objects, notwithstanding the ease with which they can inspire interest and promote engagement among visitors. Beyond being hands-on exhibits, and objects that can be fully encountered in some cases – for example, tanks at the Tank Museum, Bovington (Dorset), which visitors can climb into, and on certain days of the year travel in – these have an academic value. The values and importance of crashed military aircraft are perhaps the best understood and articulated to date, following research primarily by Holyoak (2001, 2002; English Heritage 2002). Holyoak (2002, 661-2) summarises the arguments for significance, beyond just being collectible historic artefacts, for components of any of the twenty-one types of military aircraft in use over the UK up to 1945 of which there are now no complete or substantially complete preserved examples.

The argument is often made that contemporary plans, technical publications and photographs will be useful, and provide information which would minimise the academic potential of artefacts. However there remain gaps in understanding for which the physical evidence provides an unique archive. As Holyoak (2002) states, at a basic level original components can provide information on materials and manufacturing processes, or through reverse engineering act as patterns, all of which are essential for understanding aircraft design and construction, and ensuring the accuracy of future restorations and reproductions. In a few cases the crashed remains themselves will offer the last chance to preserve relatively intact examples of aircraft previously thought extinct. An example is the recovery of virtually complete Handley Page Halifaxes from Lakes Hoklingen and Mjosa, Norway, in 1973 and 1995. The air war was characterised by intensive aircraft development, meaning that many sub-variants existed for most aircraft types – there were twenty-two sub-variants of the Vickers-Supermarine

2. The matériel culture of modern conflict

Spitfire, for example, between 1938 and 1946, and between Mks I and V alone there were thirty-five major modifications (Cotter 2001, 52). So, even for relatively common types of aircraft particular sub-variants may be especially rare. This is also true of particular components, which may be rare independent of the airframe in which they were carried.

The issues relating to later – Cold War – aircraft are slightly different. These were produced in smaller numbers and have fared better in terms of preservation, with intact examples of all major types surviving. This is because the higher cost of producing new aircraft means that existing airframes were more likely to be successively upgraded and modified than replaced, with the result that many remained in service longer than their predecessors. For these and other reasons (see English Heritage 2002, 5 for more details), crash-sites of the post-war period are thought to have less archaeological merit than earlier examples.

In recognising these components as archaeological sites and monuments as opposed to just tradeable military objects, two further considerations have relevance. First is the fact that all aircraft and aircraft crash sites (and we will keep with this example, though it applies equally to vessels and vehicles), regardless of their rarity as a type, variant and so on, offer primary data on internal fittings and equipment, colour schemes and finishing techniques, field modifications, repairs and adaptations which together demonstrate their operational use. This information has value in providing a check on documentary and oral historical data, as well as a precise and unique reference to the equipment used at a particular point in time, and in a way that preserved examples, with their long history of modification, cannot (ibid., 662). In other words, the crashed aircraft, if excavated properly, can yield information about wartime operational conditions, repair strategies and the urgency of the efforts involved in making aircraft airworthy. No other sources can provide this information.

Second – and specific to crashed aircraft and sunken vessels – is the poignancy attached to their remains, in terms of the veterans engaging with their pasts, the relatives of those killed, and the relevance of these remains to local communities, either in the vicinity of an aircrash, or the victims' place of origin. As Holyoak has noted (ibid., 662; but see also Holyoak and Saunders 2004), these sites of loss have been used in a diversity of ways for purposes of commemoration and remembrance: upland crash sites with surface wreckage have become the focal points for memorials, while excavation has sometimes been the catalyst for commemoration (Legendre 2001). It is largely for this reason perhaps that excavation has held a particular fascination for members of the general public, with the two aircraft crash site excavations filmed as part of Channel 4's Time Team attracting 2-3.5 million viewers.

Artefacts

Artefacts – whether guns, uniforms, badges and medals, barbed wire, or the mundane domestic evidence for human activity on military sites – forms a significant component of the archaeology of modern warfare. Conventionally artefacts have played their most significant role in terms of museum display, either in contributing to a generalised materiality of warfare (such as in the Imperial War Museum's exhibits), conveying a specific and often highly politicised or emotional narrative (as with the exhibits at various Holocaust museums, e.g. Weinberg and Elieli 1995), or in conveying pride, ownership and heritage in the various regimental museums. Artefacts were in each of these cases typically presented for display and education; to provide a material manifestation of certain facts; and in some cases to provide for reinterpretation or deconstruction of well-

2. The matériel culture of modern conflict

known episodes or events. But artefacts have more recently come to support more critical and experiential, more reflexive, interpretations of this recent past. Two examples make this point.

First, that meaning can be intensely personal, and more a matter of personal significance and family attachment. Also, that objects – once socially constituted – can transcend the traditional barriers set up within our society between objects and things. This theoretical stance provides the basis for Joy's (2002) analysis of his grandfather's DFC (Distinguished Flying Cross), awarded in World War II, an analysis that sees the medal remaining within the family after his grandfather's death, providing the catalyst for remembrance and reminiscence, and having a history – including possible theft within the family – that created tension and dispute. A story is told of the author's family between World War II and the writing of Joy's essay in 2001, a story that would not otherwise have been told or understood had it not been for the medal or, following its disappearance, the replica. As Joy concludes, these personal

> things play an active role within our society, just like human beings ... once constituted by performative acts they are able to communicate to us certain aspects of the personalities of dead ancestors and they can act to create and maintain social relationships (2002, 142).

Some of these connections between object and society and remembering are recognised also in the construction and treatment of so-called trench-art, the (predominantly) shells and shell-cases transformed during World War I by combatants into art objects, which were then either sold or sent home and retained by their families. Many remain within those families today (Saunders, N. 2002b). The social context here is described succinctly by Gell (1998, 74), who notes how 'decorative patterns attached to artefacts attach people to things, and to the social projects those things entail'.

Saunders describes the emergence and treatment of trench-art in three phases. Creation was during the period 1914-19, the time in which soldiers and civilians created objects that reflected the immediacy of the war, of personal injury and loss, and for some civilians a degree of economic deprivation. As Saunders states, at this time the agent of destruction was transformed physically and symbolically into something economically positive by those peoples whose lives it had shattered. Some shellcases were decorated behind the lines in safety, for example by the Royal Engineers, or Belgian metalsmiths. Others were decorated by soldiers in front-line trenches and dugouts. Others still were made by French and Belgian civilians, many of whom were refugees from devastated areas. Shellcases here could be sold as souvenirs to help make ends meet.

From 1920 to 1939 trench-art made its way into the homes of those most affected by the War, becoming treasured mementoes, set within domestic space and transformed into household ornaments. Brass shellcase vases accommodated themselves to the emotional atmosphere of a home that had suffered loss (ibid., 35), while the frequency of polishing had therapeutic quality for the bereaved.

Since 1939 and particularly in recent times these objects have become

a mainstay of the militaria trade ... . Regarded variously as antiques, militaria, souvenirs, bric-a-brac, and curiosities; the qualities of completeness, distinctiveness and shiny appearance have replaced earlier emotional values (ibid., 36).

Artefacts therefore have various meanings and roles to play

in understanding and assessing modern warfare and conflict. There are the often quite personal values that attach to certain objects, as well as the commercial and educational values which become significant as artefacts are given importance or selected for display. As museums come under increased pressure over what they collect and retain, a wider review of the values attached to these military archaeological artefacts appears timely.

Voices and words

Voices and words, or more specifically the oral historical information supplied by veterans, presented usually as first-hand accounts and diaries, are invaluable both in understanding recent and contemporary sites, and giving colour to their interpretation. I make a distinction between these sources of evidence in terms of the degrees of engagement they provide: that watching and/or hearing a veteran describe his part in a battle, or his operational role in a technologically sophisticated environment in situ, has a greater impact and more immediacy, and is more engaging than the words can ever be on their own. Television programmes often benefit from this immediacy, and the impact it provides, returning veterans to former places of work to describe the buildings, their sense of place on returning, the significance of the ambiguous and the otherwise unexplained, and to exchange views and interpretations with other veterans, sometimes former enemies.

A few years ago I attended a conference on the Battle of Britain at which two speakers were a former RAF and a former Luftwaffe fighter pilot. They each spoke for about twenty minutes about their experiences, and afterwards the press took advantage of the opportunity by encouraging handshakes and an embrace, which featured in several newspapers as well as in the published conference proceedings (Addison and Crang

2000). But what was refreshing was the exchange of opinions, about how the Luftwaffe or the RAF were not aware of the precise capabilities of each others' aircraft, and each of the two former pilots teasing the other about this.

Another example is a recent English Heritage funded project designed to record the physical legacy of the Cold War missile testing range at Spadeadam (Cumbria). Here a conventional archaeological survey has been undertaken, but of a site where some finer (including social) details were unexplained. The project has also therefore drawn on the expertise of and contacts made by a local museum to engage former employees in this recording and interpretation exercise. Veterans were also filmed visiting the now redundant buildings and offering insight into their form and function, and their emotional response on returning. This oral historical record forms an integral part of the overall historic archaeology of the site, as well as being included within a video installation created by the artist Louise K. Wilson (forthcoming).

Words themselves have value in documenting the overall social historical context of warfare. They convey what people felt at the time; what occupied their minds on the eve of battle, or during those long-drawn-out periods when nothing very much was happening. These records take the form of diaries, letters, war poems and literature (novels and autobiographies) written after the event but based directly upon personal experience.

Historical records

The relationship between archaeology as a material form of evidence for past human activity, and text is well documented, for example by Moreland in this series (2001). Indeed Moreland begins with a quote from Vermeule is which he describes 'the Word [as being] generally felt to be more powerful than, as well as cleaner than, the Dirt' (1996, 2). Here I want to make two points: first, that documentary sources and historical writing each provide valuable historical information about the past, though there are some limitations on the availability of written accounts of conflict and militarisation in recent times; and second, that rather than seeing these in opposition, for this subject in particular, recent research has demonstrated just how closely related the sources (Word and Dirt) are for purposes of analysis and interpretation.

First is the obvious point that documentary sources and historical writing are two very distinct things, which each contribute separately to our understanding of the past. Documentary sources are the primary sources created at the time and selectively retained and stored for future reference. In England many of the most significant and meaningful records derive from government departments or related non-governmental organisations. The records exist in files that are selectively retained (decisions being taken by the parent departments and institutions) and deposited in public records at the National Archives (formerly the Public Record Office). These records contain details on almost every aspect of public life, from personal records in the form of birth, marriage and death records, to the award of medals, to information on social policy, economics and military strategy. These records are typically comprehensive, detailed and accurate. They can also cover all levels of decision-making and operations. For World War II, for example, papers of the War Cabinet are available for consultation, alongside those records generated at Command level and by the individual units in the form of the Operations Records Books (RAF) and War Diaries (Army). Like all records, however, they need to be correctly and thoroughly researched: as we have seen, the distinction would need to be recognised, for example, between records that describe military sites that were built, and those that were intended but never constructed. Provided they are correctly interpreted, these records are invaluable. They provide detailed information at all levels from War Cabinet, to Command, to the local implementation of strategic operations. They cover precisely what was built, where, when and why, and often also how sites were used and by whom.

There is one significant drawback, at least in the UK, and that is the Thirty Year Rule, which means that files will remain closed for thirty years, and possibly for much longer, depending on sensitivities about what they contain. Most sources for the study of World War II are now available for public scrutiny and research (see Dobinson et al. 1997 for an example of what can be achieved from consulting these sources), but for the Cold War only files closed before 1974 are currently available, and given political sensitivities some earlier material also remains closed. This element of secrecy adds to that imposed by the Official Secrets Act, meaning that some information will remain unobtainable through official channels, thus placing a greater burden on field archaeological evidence to provide interpretation. This was discussed briefly at the end of Chapter 1.

Historical writing takes many forms, from histories written after the event, and potentially at least politically spun towards a particular interpretation of past events, to official histories written at the time and by official – government sponsored – historians and journalists. This is not the place for a critical review of each. Suffice to say that all have value, but do require some critical appraisal if they are to be used effectively for historical (re)interpretation. Official histories are a case in point. Often produced by parent government departments, these bear all the hallmarks of a credible, comprehensive and informed study of, say, Britain at war in 1939-40. Yet to appreciate fully their significance and their validity as historic documents requires an understanding of their intended purpose and audience. Were they written to promote or boost morale, for example, and if so what was being held back? To give an example, none of the official histories describing Britain at war made any mention of bombing decoys, for the same reason that each of the 800 or so decoys constructed in remote areas of the UK were cordoned off, being secretive and restricted places even to those that lived nearby (Dobinson 2000a). As these were effectively created as new targets for enemy bombers, it is easy to understand why.

Written records are a significant source therefore, and constitute a specific form of material culture that requires very particular skills for interpretation. But the real advantage of these records – when used correctly – is how they can complement physical archaeological remains. For bombing decoys, for example, documentary sources revealed how many were built, precisely where they were located, and what form they took (i.e. whether day or night dummy aerodromes – the so-called 'K' or 'Q' sites; diversionary fires ['QF' sites or Starfish]; simulated urban lighting ['QL' sites]; or dummy factories and buildings [Dobinson 2000a]). The complementary use of field evidence included a study of aerial photographs from 1946 onwards to locate each of these sites and determine what – if anything – still survives, in order to inform future management priorities (Dobinson 2000a, 214ff.; Schofield 2002a). This work confirmed the low rates of survival: only 1.6% of the decoys survived in anything like their original form, as legible sites with fire-break trenches that contained the simulated fires, and control buildings, and only a few more where only the buildings survive without any trace of the decoy itself. This and the related studies of anti-aircraft sites, coast batteries and radar stations are unique in providing both the original population of a monument class and its current rates of survival (Schofield 2002a). The erosion trajectory can be easily reconstructed for all classes of wartime sites using historic aerial photographs. (See also Thomas 2003 for an example of this methodology applied to World War II prisoner of war camps in England.)

Photographs and film

Imagery is one of the most effective media for conveying the conditions of war. It was used in the Boer War, and indeed to a very limited extent even in the Crimea 150 years ago. But it has been used routinely since World War I, and took on renewed significance in the second Gulf War with live 'real time' coverage bringing the war directly into the living rooms and lives of people around the world. This instantaneous communication, and its ability to transport everyone into front-line conflict, and to witness the sights and sounds of battle, can have dramatic effects. It may serve to promote anti-war sentiment, but it also has value in communicating to all a human condition that until recently few have witnessed and which few could therefore fully understand. The role of journalists 'embedded' within military units will surely continue to have this significance in the longer term.

Pictures of the fallen and of battlefield topography in World War I are a common feature of museums along the Front, and they provide a highly charged and effective medium for conveying a spatial and social context for the words referred to earlier. Pictures taken by the liberating army of concentration camps in 1945 have a similar effect. As Roland Barthes has so eloquently said: 'I ... explore [photographs] not as a question, but as a wound: I see, I feel, hence I notice, I observe, and I think' (2000, 21). We have all experienced this I'm sure: we see a line of photographs in an exhibition, or a collection published as a book, and on reading them through most are inert under our gaze (ibid.), but once in a while a photograph pricks us (Barthes refers to this quality as the punctum [the accident of the picture that bruises and has poignancy]). Photographs provide insight in a deep, detailed and often quite provocative way. But perhaps the main value of photographs over other sources of information is that – excepting some instances of 'trick imagery'

2. The matériel culture of modern conflict

– photographs demonstrate presence; that something was/is
real. Barthes describes a picture of Polish soldiers resting in a
field in 1915. As he observes, there is nothing extraordinary
about that, except that *they were there* (emphasis in original);
'what I see is not a memory, an imagination, a reconstruction,
a piece of Maya, such as art lavishes upon us, but reality in a
past state: at once the past and the real' (2000, 82).

Artistic expression

The twentieth century has witnessed a cultural trend towards
depersonalisation, yet within the material records of war and
industrialisation, for example, and now globalisation, there
remain traces that constitute a very intimate record. We have
already described words, photographs and objects that reflect
this personalised record of a century of conflict, but artistic
expression is also worth emphasising, both for its diversity and
for its significance in enabling and articulating human responses to war and conflict. There are many examples of this,
but I will mention only two: wall art of World War II and the
Cold War period (English Heritage 2004a), and beyond, and
art's inspirational qualities in generating current interpretations of and commentaries on the past.

Graffiti and doodlings on walls have long been features of
military establishments and places occupied by military personnel. In World War II this became more formalised, for
example through the generation of nose-art on aeroplanes, and
unit insignia on flying jackets. Distinctions were clearly drawn
between artwork in public spaces (e.g. morale-boosting murals
and insignia) and private (where instructional drawing might
occur in technical areas, alongside pin-ups). Some images are
vast, and some tiny; some are in bold colours, spray-painted
onto walls, and others are pencil sketches. Contrast Mickey and
Minnie Mouse painted on a prisoner of war camp wall in

Lincolnshire, with Death holding a depleted uranium round, at RAF Bentwaters (Suffolk), for example, and 'Our Target for Tonight' from the Falklands War era (Figure 2.4). The significance of this wall art is that it can offer insight into the culture of different armed forces (English Heritage 2004). Wall art on British (RAF) bases, for example, is quite restrained compared to the bold and often overtly aggressive 'Street-Gangsta' cartoon styles found on many United States Air Force bases. A greater contrast still is found with the formulaic and politically ordained wall art found in Warsaw Pact countries, and between art on the bases and that created by those opposed to military deployment, and their presence sometimes on land traditionally owned by others. In the Nevada Desert, for example, a diverse protest community has generated a symbolic landscape made up of rock-lined images and signs depicting the various religious communities from which they derive: thus Franciscan crosses sit alongside stars of David, feminist symbols, peace signs, Christian and Buddhist signs and so on (Schofield et al. 2003).

The social and interpretive value of this material culture (Cocroft and Schofield 2003; Cocroft and Thomas 2003, 74-5) includes both contemporary wall art and that introduced following a base's closure and abandonment. As archaeologists interpreting the history of occupation and use, for us graffiti and wall art – whether we consider it vandalism or not – forms part of the site's narrative, and should be interpreted, in much the same way as few of us would now sanction the complete removal of everything post-medieval on an excavation in order to reach the 'more interesting' earlier material. So, how do we view 1960s graffiti – beautifully painted and striking imagery for the most part – depicting party scenes, in buildings previously occupied as an early twentieth-century mobilisation centre south of London? Equally – and rather more provocatively – how do we assess the sexually explicit scenes painted

Fig. 2.4. 'Our Target for Tonight': wall art from the Falklands War.

(again to a high standard of representation) on walls of the now protected former RAF station at Bempton in East Yorkshire (Dearing 2002)? These have been linked to devil-worship and the occult, hidden away in this remote and underground place above the cliffs of East Yorkshire. They are explicit, dark and disturbing. Should they be preserved as part of the narrative at this significant wartime radar station? Or should they be painted over? Does 'quality' have anything to do with it?

Finally, there is the inspirational quality of these military sites, and the fact that these places are themselves inspiring a new record specifically with the purpose of questioning and challenging those who encounter them. This is a record that draws explicitly on the experiences of the past, in the form of installation art, photographic essays, poetry and music.

Perhaps best known of the many examples is the Turner-nominated Wilson twins' video sculpture GAMMA, recorded and filmed at Greenham Common airbase. This installation investigates the themes of power, surveillance and paranoia through photographs, performance and installation art (Schjeldahl 1999). The art critic Matthew Collings describes GAMMA thus:

> The silo still exists [at Greenham Common's GAMA site] and [the Wilson twins] filmed it without changing any-thing. Scenes of its grungy, dilapidated interiors go by as if shot by surveillance cameras – that is, in a disconnected way. But at the same time connected by suggestions and atmospheres. The main suggestion is of an exploration of alienated selfhood in the context of science fiction horror film. So it's not really a surveillance film but it might express contemporary fears of surveillance and it's not fiction because the silo is real. So it's a fake masquerading as a fiction or vice versa. In any case, the comment doesn't

seem to be that we should all breathe a sigh of relief that the cruise missiles have gone (1999, 57).

Greenham was also the inspiration for John Kippin's photographic essay *Cold War Pastoral* (2001), which documented the changing landscape of Greenham as it reverted to common land, and Michael Symmonds Roberts' book of poetry *Burning Babylon* (2001). Most recently the Cold War was the inspiration for Yannis Kyriakides' musical composition *a conSPIracy cantata*, performed in the Debrief Centre or Star Wars Building at Bentwaters airbase (Suffolk) as part of the 2002 Aldeburgh Festival. Louise K. Wilson's work at Spadeadam (in press) is a further example of this approach to interpreting the recent past, as is Angus Boulton's study of an abandoned Soviet base in eastern Germany, *Cood bay Forst Zinna* (2001), and Frank Watson's *The Hush House* (2004).

As I have said elsewhere (Cocroft and Schofield 2003, 44), both contemporary wall art and later representations of the Cold War, inspired by front-line bases, demonstrate the link between experience and imaginative response in a way that other sources cannot achieve. In transforming the redundant spaces of Cold War military bases, art can usefully create a dialogue between the past and the present. It can serve also as an eloquent expression of opposing views, between East and West, military and political authorities and the peace movement. Artistic representation can also play a significant role in increasing public understanding of the physical remains of war.

Summary

This chapter has provided an overview of the sources of evidence for interpreting the material culture of recent conflict, and to some extent the recent and contemporary pasts in general. It has highlighted the obvious point that landscape is the appropriate scale at which to examine the cultural effects of warfare, while material culture of various kinds also provides the evidence for interpretation to be socially constructed and personal. The point is also made implicitly throughout that these sources are best viewed in combination. Finally, it is obvious that using numerous of these sources (e.g. documentary sources, oral history, artefacts) requires particular skills and judgements, and the study of recent conflict will therefore inevitably be trans-disciplinary in scope. However, the nature of our enquiry, the types of question described here and the manner in which we are seeking to interpret and deconstruct past human activity constitutes what I consider a uniquely archaeological approach. I regard this is a subject which lends itself to study with an archaeological mindset, focused on human conditions, social context and experience. We might draw upon the expertise of others in the fields of history, historic geography, art and art history, science and technology, museum studies and those with a military background for advice and support, and to pursue some of the research themes identified briefly in the chapter, but I contend that the approach is essentially an archaeological one. I shall return to this again.

3

Memory and meaning

This third chapter explores the middle and largely theoretical ground that exists between the monuments and material culture of war and the ways in which they are variously preserved, recorded and presented within contemporary society. This chapter therefore explores the motivations that underlie management decision-making, whether by heritage professionals or the communities among which these places and objects now survive. In that sense it is also about public archaeology and ownership of the past.

I will begin by outlining briefly some of the ways in which values and perceptions are identified and given meaning, and the different levels within society at which judgments are made. I will then review some of the conceptual frameworks within which those decisions are taken. These various frameworks – ranging from the more obvious and predictable (e.g. remembrance, understanding, retribution) to the less obvious and less well understood (discord value) – are presented and critically assessed through case studies. The management options themselves, decided subsequently, and approaches to preservation and re-use, form the subject of Chapter 4.

Values and meaning: what matters, why and to whom

It is generally accepted that all places have value, that many different people and social groups will ascribe values to places, that value is judgmental and either subjective or objective or both, and that those values are numerous and diverse (see, e.g., de la Torre 2002; Byrne et al. 2001). The various ways in which recent military sites hold significance will be addressed in the following sections, but first it is important to stress that recent remains are not quite as common as some might think; that our value judgments are being ascribed to an ever-diminishing resource. The discussion begins therefore by considering rarity before going on to review the various levels within society at which significance is defined, and the reasons why these sites should be valued. Why these places matter and to whom, in other words.

Rarity and risk

Much of the archaeological resource is at risk (e.g. Darvill and Fulton 1998; Accardo et al. 2003), a risk that is just as real and significant for monuments of the recent and contemporary past as it is for earlier periods (e.g. Anderton and Schofield 1999). Let us consider a well-documented example. The English Heritage-commissioned Monuments at Risk Survey noted that at least 16% of all recorded monuments in England no longer exist, nearly half of that loss being the result of damage and wholesale destruction over the last fifty years. In terms of losses to land area with recorded archaeological deposits, approximately 44% of land known to contain such deposits had been destroyed by 1995 (Darvill and Fulton 1998, 244). Also commissioned by English Heritage was the Twentieth Century Fortifications in England project (Dobinson et al. 1997; Dobinson 2000a, 2001) in which documentary sources were studied to reveal the original populations for and distributions of all major classes of World War II monuments (e.g. anti-aircraft gunsites). This study was followed by another that investigated all the documented locations to determine what survived at these places fifty to sixty years later. Even for monument classes as recent as these – and in most cases these are classes that have potential to be as robust and substantial now as when they were first built – the rates of survival are surprisingly small. In a review of these survival statistics I have summarised the findings and given some explanation for them (Schofield 2002a; the survival of World War II bombing decoys and anti-aircraft sites is also discussed in Dobinson 2000a and 2001 respectively). To demonstrate rarity of these recent remains it is worth restating some of the most significant results of this study.

To begin with heavy anti-aircraft gunsites, these were substantially built sites, generally covering large areas and to a standard design. The sites therefore had a distinctive plan form, with each containing concrete access roads, four or eight large concrete emplacements for heavy guns, hutting for domestic accommodation and numerous other buildings (see Dobinson 2001 for details). Yet of the thousand or so sites built in England during World War II only ten are known to survive in their original form with all of these components intact. An additional forty-seven are substantially complete and remain legible; fragments survive at a further 119 sites. But at 790 sites there is now no surface trace, only fifty to sixty years since their abandonment. Not surprisingly post-war use has aided preservation (Schofield 2002a, 275). Of the 192 World War II heavy anti-aircraft sites selected for post-war use as the so-called Cold War 'Nucleus Force', thirty (16% of the total) survive as either complete or substantially complete examples; only 6% of those not selected for Cold War use have survived.

Diver sites were heavy and light anti-aircraft gunsites designed specifically to counter the threat of the flying bomb to British cities in 1944-5. Again these are distinctive sites, all examples of which have been located through documentary research (Dobinson 1996b). The rates of survival are again low.

Of the 1,190 sites located by documentary study, only nine are recorded as being either complete or substantially complete and seventy-two have fragmentary survival. Over 90% of these sites have now been removed, leaving at best only fragmented buried remains. As flying bombs were launched at Britain from various places at different times, the response needed to be flexible and highly mobile. Light guns reflect that mobility better than the heavy guns, which had more or less permanent emplacements. This is also reflected in the survival of these sites today with barely any of this ephemeral light gun deployment surviving.

Finally, there are regional variations in survival. Given the inclement winter weather, sites on England's east coast were more substantially built to provide better accommodation for troops. Thus in the south-east of England only 6% of heavy anti-aircraft *Diver* sites survive, contrasting with 40% on the east coast.

Proportionately more examples of coast batteries and radar stations survive. For coast batteries this is because earlier (and 'historic') coastal fortifications were often re-armed in World War II, and these later additions survive as part of the historic fabric, representing continuity of purpose (this recycling of military 'brownfield' sites may become more common as the MoD estate is reduced). In all only 19% of the sites constructed prior to 1921 have now been removed, compared with 61% of those (Emergency Batteries) constructed in the period 1938-45 (Schofield 2002a, 278). Radar stations also survive comparatively well, and for similar reasons to the Nucleus Force anti-aircraft gunsites. In all, 57% of the 242 radar stations used in World War II survive in one form or another, the reason for this comparatively high figure again being their continued use and adaptation during the Cold War period (ibid., 272-3).

This study therefore makes the point, outlined also in the Monuments at Risk Survey (MARS), that despite being recent,

3. Memory and meaning

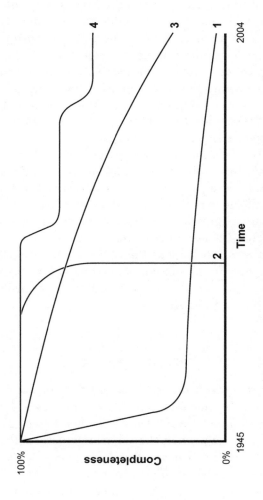

Fig. 3.1. Decay curve of wartime airfields.

1   Largely cleared at end of war, but stabilised in its abandoned and fragmented state.
2   Remained operational into Cold War before clearance and redevelopment.
3   Abandonment in 1945, and agricultural use/storage thereafter.
4   Continued in use before being twice adapted for new use, the result of
    changes in defence strategy and technological development.

85

robust and substantial constructions, such military sites cannot be considered commonplace. Like MARS, this study has also revealed the decay curve and the causes of removal. As the MARS report states (citing Groube and Bowden 1982), the life-cycle of a monument class can be visualised graphically as a decay curve extending along an axis representing time as calculable from the date of construction. The decay curve typically begins steeply but shallows as components stabilise in relation to their surroundings (Darvill and Fulton 1998, 16). For these World War II monuments the decay curve can take any of a variety of forms (see Figure 3.1).

The decay curve profiles and the causes of decay for these recent military monuments are thus varied, and overall a surprisingly small percentage of the sites survives. It is logical that greater significance is therefore placed on those few surviving sites, though recognising also that memory can be invested in place even once the building or site has gone.

Before going on to describe the various motivations for seeking to retain these recent monuments, I will also briefly discuss some of the constituencies involved, and their potential connectivity with the contemporary past.

'Anoraks' and significant others – defining constituents

The Oxford Dictionary describes an 'anorak' as a socially inept person with unfashionable and solitary interests. I was once asked to speak live on a local radio station about the defence heritage. It was only when the programme started and I was awaiting my cue that I heard the announcer refer to the programme as 'Anorak Hour'! Perhaps it can be argued that those whose predilection is recording a specific component of a specific type of military structure (and in some cases a specific aspect of the specific component ...) can be classed as 'anoraks', but it is inappropriate to apply that label any more than we would for similar specialists in prehistoric archaeology, or medieval studies. Why, for example, should lithics specialists, some of whom may undertake research into specific aspects of tool manufacture, and on a specific type of artefact of a particular period, be described as specialists, while those whose work is equally focussed but concerned instead with modern material culture are called 'anoraks?' Perhaps the argument is more about the purpose of accumulating knowledge, though here too I fail to see any distinction between studying flaking scars on stone artefacts and the examination of holdfast bolts. I do however see a clear distinction between both of these pursuits and the collection of train numbers, car registration plates, and so on, simply for the sake of collection. There are 'anoraks' in this field of study, just as there are in prehistory; people will always want to collect lithic artefacts, just as people will want to find and 'collect' pillboxes, just for the sake of it. Here, though, it is recognised that this study has a purpose, and that most practitioners contribute to it. However, notwithstanding the semantics of this argument, 'specialists' are one constituency, and a valuable one in that their detailed and focussed research contributes to a bigger picture and a fuller understanding of the subject. As Kate Clark so eloquently states throughout her *Informed Conservation* (2001), detailed knowledge – whether of roofing materials, paint and texture of wall coverings, or holdfast bolts in a gun emplacement – is an essential prerequisite for informed conservation and management planning.

Veterans' groups and former scientists, combatants and those for whom conflict had some social or economic relevance also have significance here. All can contribute to knowledge and understanding, for example of the conditions of war, and of the science and civil engineering that underlie Research and Development programmes (e.g. Walley 2001). But more significantly,

I think, all can claim some ownership of this recent past. Take the example of the Torbay slipways, Torquay. These two slips represent perhaps the single most spectacular surviving example of monumental architecture relating to the D-Day embarkation of June 1944. American troops embarked here en route for Utah and Omaha Beaches at which they suffered heavy losses. Prior to an English Heritage survey of these D-Day preparatory sites (Dobinson 1996c; Schofield 2001) little was known about them, how many survived and how well, and what role they played in the history of the D-Day landings. That information now exists, but came at an unfortunate time for Torquay Harbour, for which a regeneration scheme had just been produced at the time the significance of the slips was first realised. This scheme involved demolition of the slips, which English Heritage then listed in order to protect them. The point here is that this was not a campaign pursued by the national heritage agency in isolation. Every four years the Normandy Veterans hold a commemoration service at the head of the slips, and they too argued strongly for preservation (as – it is rumoured – did Steven Spielberg, then in England filming *Band of Brothers*). It is now hoped that the slips will be retained within the context of a revised harbour regeneration scheme.

The defence heritage is now a significant addition to the professional fields of military history, archaeology and heritage (e.g. Dobinson 2000a, 2001; Cocroft 2001; Cocroft and Thomas 2003; Schofield at al. 2002; Schofield 2004). The subject has become a serious academic pursuit in and across numerous disciplines including archaeology, art history, history and geography (political, economic, military and social), anthropology and sociology. It is also a subject that has immense support among local communities who recognise the value of military (among other recent) heritage sites in constructing their senses of self, place and identity. Places of tragedy are especially relevant here, and will inevitably inspire and imbue a sense of personal attachment and cultural relevance and meaning, such as with Holocaust sites (Gilbert 1998).

Finally here is the degree of public support and interest, as reflected in the plethora of television programmes covering military archaeology, the numbers of viewers these attract, the numbers of visitors to historic sites, and the appetite there appears to be for books and films, fact and fiction. It is a popular subject for a diversity of interest groups.

Social significance and intangible heritage

Much of what I have described so far has been the physical traces, the material legacy in the form of objects, pictures or monuments of war. In this section and at times in the next chapter I want to drop the distinction between these physical or tangible traces and what is referred to as intangible heritage: in this case referring to the sense of past events and occupancy; the 'ghosts of place' as Bell (1997) has described it. I will do this for two reasons: first, because this is a recent and familiar past and the landscape will therefore inevitably be loaded with memories and meanings for those that still inhabit it, whether these are first- or second-hand; and secondly because the distinction between tangible and intangible remains is questionable in any case. As archaeologists, anthropologists, visitors to unfamiliar places or occupants of familiar ones, we inevitably and continually read the landscape, we interpret it and construct meaning within it. Some of these meanings and interpretations have physical expression (such as a plaque, a memorial or a physical monument such as an air raid shelter), and some do not (such as the place where an air raid shelter once was). Drawing all this together is the knowledge and insight of the person reading that landscape, and as is always the case – whether what survives is tangible or not – interpretation will be personalised and related directly to personal experience.

Given how few sites of this period now survive in tangible form, the memory of long-gone sites and the continued meaning of the place, the 'site of ...', for some has equal strength and validity. Peter Read has discussed this at length, referring to these places as 'inspirited'. In *Returning to Nothing* (1996) he described the emotions felt by people returning to significant places where all physical trace has gone. With cultural studies (and including studies of cultural heritage) now beginning to focus more on the individual in society, this personal attachment to place (and in Read's case specifically *lost* places) becomes more important. As he says, 'Memories are ghosts that won't lie down' (1996, 200), which makes it easy to understand why veterans return to the stations from which they flew, and focus their commemorative energy on the control tower, the most iconic of airfield buildings, and the one from which aircraft were counted out and counted back. And this is also why it is easy to recognise the significance of the loss of such buildings, effectively removing the object of commemoration.

Much of what I describe here is referred to by Byrne et al. (2001) as 'social significance'. As the authors state in their introduction:

Individuals and communities are engaged in an endless conversation with the landscapes in which they live. One side of this conversation involves people giving meaning to places through the events in their lives which have 'taken place' in them. Generations pass knowledge of these events down to each other. Often the events have left no mark on the places, no mark on the landscape, but people remember what has happened. ... When we walk through our landscapes the sight of a place will often trigger the memories and the feelings – good or bad, happy or sad – which go with them. This is the other side of the conversation: the landscape talking to us. ... Heritage practitioners

[can only discover this world of meaning] by talking to
people (ibid., 3).

Another dimension is provided by Mason:

> Social value ... includes the 'place attachment' aspects of
> heritage value. Place attachment refers to the social cohe-
> sion, community identity, or other feelings of affiliation
> that social groups (whether very small and local, or na-
> tional in scale) derive from the specific heritage and
> environment characteristics of their 'home' territory
> (2002, 12).

There are two points here. First, that the recent and contemporary pasts provide the opportunity for developing this approach
and engaging communities directly with their historic landscape, and the military heritage within it. Communities do feel
a strong sense of attachment to their military past. Numerous
cases have arisen in recent years of planning decisions that
involve the removal of a pillbox or some other defence structure.
Particularly with World War II examples, this immediately
creates an opposition between the applicant and the community
whose letters of support for what are generally ugly and unap-
pealing structures are impassioned and heartfelt. David Hunt
describes an example arising from a British Army Regiment
occupying former Wehrmacht barracks in Germany, which
were renamed from the original Von Bulow Kaserne. It was
suggested that a notice be included under the new regimental
sign mentioning this fact. There was opposition from the Army,
though the German press welcomed the move, as did the German regiment that had occupied the barracks in the 1930s.

Second is the value of oral historical evidence, not only from
those involved with combat, but those also that it impacted
upon, and who dealt with its consequences. In the case of a

crashed military aircraft, for example, this oral historical approach could usefully take account not only of survivors and their descendents, and those involved in the crash recovery, the victims' friends and family, but also those in the local community. In Australia's Cape York, for example, World War II sites – including crashed aircraft – have cross-cultural significance to local Aboriginal communities, for whom they are absorbed now into memory and the intangible heritage of these communities. The spirits of those killed aboard crashed aircraft 'inhabit' the landscape (Greer et al. 2002, 273), and there are traditional dances that reflect the experiences of the period of loss (McIntyre-Tamwoy 2002, 175-6). In a sense this also returns to the point made in the previous chapter by Barthes, concerning the picture of Polish soldiers, the photograph proving that they were there: just one snapshot in the wider war, but one that captures one moment in one place that will evermore have significance for that reason. The landscape has changed to such an extent that the place will never be known, but it exists somewhere, and had meaning for those soldiers and especially for the photographer, later for Barthes when he selected this example (even though he doesn't reproduce the image), and again by my including the reference here. Places matter, for different reasons, at different levels of significance (and judged or defined by a diversity of criteria) and to different people. I will now review these various motivations.

Motivations

Preserving to remember, and to not forget

This section examines the connections that exist between memory on the one hand, and on the other those objects and places used as a means of recognising the material legacies of war as having importance for constructing memory and re (or de)constructing imagined and real pasts. This is a complex area, which can only be outlined here. Two citations illustrate the complexity. First, Kuchler (1999) who agrees with de Certeau (1984) in stating that recollection does not cease when there are no longer any traces of what is to be remembered, but draws its force from this absence. And second, her co-editor of *The Art of Forgetting* (1999), who noted in his introduction that:

> The Western tradition of memory since the Renaissance has been founded upon the assumption that material objects, whether natural or artificial, can act as the analogues of human memory. It has been generally taken for granted that memories formed in the mind can be transferred to solid material objects, which can come to stand for memories and, by virtue of their durability, either prolong or preserve them indefinitely beyond their purely mental existence (Forty 1999, 2).

Forty's excellent introduction to this important collection of essays goes on to provide three examples that indicate a difficulty with the assumed clarity of this relationship between object and memory.

The first comprises ephemeral monuments, non-Western artefacts with apparently memorial purposes, but which are made only to be abandoned immediately to decay. These may be interpreted as a means by which members of society get rid of what they no longer need or wish to remember, or where 'their brief exposure acts as a momentary confirmation of what everybody within the culture already knows, but of which otherwise they have no need to be reminded' (ibid., 5).

The second example concerns Freud's theory of mental processes in which he stressed that forgetting is often intentional and desired. In a sense the purpose of psychoanalysis for him was not a memory cure, but rather aimed to provide the patient with the means truly to forget the repressed material of which they were the victim. 'As Freud once remarked, the aim was to give the patients the "freedom to decide one way or the other", whether to remember or forget' (ibid., 5). Thus physical artefacts could not be regarded as analogues of memory, because 'mental material was not subject to the same processes of decay as objects in the phenomenal world' (ibid., 6).

The third reason given by Forty relates to Holocaust sites, and the 'realization that conventional memorial practices were inadequate and inappropriate to the task' (ibid.). The dilemma here is a simple one:

> As the greatest atrocity of modern times, the natural reaction to its unbearable memory was to forget – which is exactly what many of the survivors themselves did, or attempted to do. Yet, as they and everyone else knew, to forget it was to risk its repetition.

Forty goes on to note how attempts to preserve the memory of the Holocaust look futile within this context, and if they take the form of artefact-making, perhaps even counter-productive.

With all of this in mind we cannot take for granted the role of artefacts and monuments, either as agents of collective memory, or for prolonging it, except by recognising that places and objects can serve to provoke memory and enable it, thus ensuring that past events are not forgotten. It is not the case therefore that objects are required to perpetuate memory, as memory can clearly stand alone, but rather that objects play a role in provoking it, prompting reflective thought and creating dialogue with the past. Objects and place are more significant in preventing amnesia therefore; they are more about not forgetting than about remembrance.

Some military places – whether sites or landscapes – saw combat, and thus fatalities; they might have seen torture or suffering and death as a result of the war. Either way these will

almost instantly become sacred places, with a particular pertinence for those whose friends and relatives are among the
deceased. In the immediate aftermath of war these are literally
places of and for remembrance: people visit the battlefields and
places of mass murder and torture, of suffering and deprivation,
specifically to remember, and to use the physicality of the
landscape, and the ruined buildings, the aura of destruction,
the scattered matériel, to imagine and through imagination to
remember past lives and personalities. Immediately after
World War I, for example, relatives wanted to visit the graves
of their sons, husbands and brothers, while after a few years
surviving soldiers wanted to return, to recall and to reflect
(Figure 3.2). Within a few years trips were common, and as a
result guidebooks began to appear, such as the Michelin
Guides, published in the 1920s and 30s and now republished in
facsimile (Michelin Guide 1994). Nearly a century later visitor
numbers continue to increase, especially now through official
channels and tour companies; visitor centres and museums sit

Fig. 3.2. A World War I cemetery in northern France.

95

alongside sacred landscapes along the former Western Front; while interpretation has become increasingly 'hot' (Uzzell 1989) and engaging as time goes on. The motivations now are many and diverse, including the recognition of battlefields alongside other categories of cultural heritage simply as places to visit for their historic value. For some it is still to remember, but that is increasingly not the case.

Gallipoli, however, does still have considerable resonance as a place of memory, and pilgrimages by Australians to witness 'the sheer awfulness of this landscape' (Scates 2002) continue. The nature of these modern day pilgrimages is of interest here, as are the motivations behind them. To give an example (after Scates 2002, 1): in Australia 'Jenny' often attended Anzac (Remembrance) Day services. They were small suburban events which she did not find very inspiring. But 25 April 1995 at Anzac Cove was another matter entirely:

> 'we arrived at about 4 am in the dark and the lapping of the waves sent shivers up one's spine … I cried when the last post sounded, as did several of my … friends. … We … stood there looking out to sea and you could almost hear the sound of battle.'
> …

Jenny had read widely before she went but 'nothing prepared me for the sheer awfulness of the landscape'. And nothing prepared her for the 'terrible sacrifice' entombed in Gallipoli's cemeteries: 'to walk along and read the names + inscriptions + ages of the soldiers makes one feel so sad'. Jenny stood in the graveyards overlooking the bright blue Aegean sea and wondered how grieving mothers 'could justify the loss of their sons in far away countries'. At Quinn's post, she found the grave of her own cousin; she 'heard "the ghosts that march up and down the gullies". I can still hear them.'

3. Memory and meaning

This sense of pilgrimage also provides the link between sacred landscapes (the object of pilgrimage) and the artefacts and personal effects (the inspiration and cause of them). As Scates has noted:

> The real history of pilgrimage takes place on a personal plane, pieced together with the fragments of fading diaries or letters. Pilgrims related what they called the relics of a young man's life, the photographs 'hung above the telephone' of an endlessly grieving grandmother, the medals prized by children each Anzac Day, the grim collection of personal effects, the final letters folded carefully in a family bible (2002, 4).

As we have seen already with the Distinguished Flying Cross of Joy's (2002) grandfather, it is these stories that breathe life into such belongings (Scates 2002, 4). It is also these stories that give meaning and significance to the landscapes in which the battles were fought.

But we should return to the distinction between remembrance (which I consider motivated by personal connections and interest in an individual or a particular unit) and not forgetting. The not forgetting of an event is a culturally constructed and defined process, and relates generally to tragedies, atrocities and actions at a more general level; events that have a broader and often more profound impact on contemporary society. Not forgetting might be the inspiration behind a conservation management plan for a Holocaust site, and the construction of a new interpretation centre that perhaps has a cathartic dimension; remembrance will remain the motivation for victims' families to visit the site, and to wish the actual place where death occurred, or where that person was last photographed on departure for the camp, to be preserved.

Finally here we should recall that the process of excavation is itself therapeutic and for many necessary as part of the process of grieving and remembering. This was one of the more significant outcomes of Legendre's (2001) excavation of a crashed Lancaster bomber at Fléville, France. It is also the rationale that underpins much of the work undertaken by the United States' Missing in Action Teams. Hoshower-Leppo (2002) described both procedures and motivations for several crashed aircraft excavations in Vietnam and Laos in pursuing the 'federally mandated task of the search for, recovery of and identification of all unaccounted-for US service members from all military conflicts and missions' (2002, 89-90).

Interpretation and remembering

A justification for retaining some military sites within a constantly changing cultural landscape is their potential specifically for the interpretation of past events. The twentieth century may be recent and well documented, but as we have seen that doesn't mean we understand it any better than we do earlier periods. The places that survive contain information that will tell us more, either by interpreting the minutiae of architectural details, or through new approaches to spatial analysis. The impact of Cold War airfields on the landscape tells us much about the scale and significance of militarisation in the post World War II period, for example.

This need to understand impact at landscape scale was partly the motivation behind a proposed Cold War Museum at Upper Heyford (Oxfordshire), England (Hinchliffe 1997). Covering 1,250 acres and divided between accommodation, service (technical) buildings and the flying field with its fifty-six hardened aircraft shelters, this was home to eighty-two F-111 fighter bombers. Following its initial use during World War II by the RAF, the base was occupied by the United States Air

Force who vacated the site in 1994. Plans for the museum followed. As the prospectus explained, this was intended to

> commemorate, celebrate, display and explore the international, social, political, economic and technical developments over the last 50 years. ... It would not be a museum or a theme park as they are commonly understood. It would have the educational purpose of the former while aspiring to the scale and popular appeal of the latter.

It goes on:

> Since the Cold War lacked battles and heroes, exhilarating advances or ignominious retreats, future generations will find it difficult to grasp its fundamental qualities unless it is recorded and explained in vivid and possibly innovative ways (1997, 234-5).

As at the Imperial War Museum at Duxford, visitors would be able to visit and examine Cold War matériel and experience the scale and sheer physical impact of militarisation in the twentieth century. As things turned out, Upper Heyford (for now at least) did not get its museum. But what is interesting is that this failure has not compromised the site's capacity to convey its size, form and impact to new occupants and visitors. Proposed plans for the site include a new settlement set within the footprint of the domestic accommodation originally provided for service personnel; business and community services within what was once the technical site; and open space, storage and leisure facilities on the former flying field, with the hardened aircraft shelters remaining dispersed around the airfield's perimeter, set partly in woodland but partly too in open space, retaining some of the characteristic airfield vistas.

The character would therefore be retained alongside beneficial new uses.

Also within the politicised context of the Cold War was the peace movement, set up in ideological opposition to the principles of the nuclear deterrent (see Pritchard 1999 for a review and Roseneil 2000 for details of Greenham Common). From studies such as Pritchard's, much is known of how the peace movement developed and evolved between the 1960s and 1990s, in the UK, the United States and elsewhere. What isn't fully known, however, at least not beyond superficial limits of the most obvious materiality of temporary encampments and protest graffiti, is the archaeology of this opposition. With such an emphasis on Cold War heritage and history, and its material culture specifically (e.g. Cocroft and Thomas 2003 for the UK; Johnson and Beck 1995 for the United States), this archaeology of opposition is a critical part of the broader archaeology of the Cold War period, emphasising the contradictions of scale and material, and the open versus closed communities that these legacies signify and represent. And this appears a critical distinction to accommodate in conservation management thinking: the militarised landscape is massively robust and extensive, covering vast areas of landscape; the peace movement survives now as small compact locations, camp sites occupied for short periods and either abandoned with residents taking away all meaningful possessions, or being forcibly removed and their homes bulldozed. This is an archaeology of transience, therefore, and the contrast with the subject of their opposition could not be more pronounced.

Two projects, one at Greenham Common (West Berkshire) and another at Peace Camp, Nevada in the United States, are beginning to explore these differences, while at the same time involving community groups in the interpretation and critical analysis of their own familiar pasts. At Nevada this work has involved the field recording of the 700 or so stone arrangements left by protesters opposed to nuclear testing programmes taking place in the desert sixty-five miles north-west of Las Vegas. These arrangements divide up into domestic accommodation (hearths, sleeping areas), way markers (cairns and rock piles) and more symbolic and artistic interventions. These artistic arrangements are perhaps the most challenging and the most interesting of remains (Figure 3.3). They represent the physical manifestations of views and beliefs, of ideologies that were often very distinct. Las Vegas is the nearest city, and here a diverse religious community provided the basis for opposition to nuclear testing. So, in the desert were Franciscans, Christians, Jews, Buddhists, feminist groups, new-age communities, and the traditional owners of this land, the Western Shoshone Indians. Also represented at various times were peace groups from around the world, and notably from Hiroshima. Stone arrangements depicting symbols for each of these groups as well as different nationalities have created a diverse and challenging material record.

As at Greenham Common, where the archaeology is more conventional, and almost Mesolithic by virtue of its transient campsites, reoccupied frequently following each eviction event (Schofield and Anderton 2000; Roseneil 2000), the point here is about recognising two things: first, that the archaeology of the Cold War in these two places is not just about events inside the fence, but on the outside too; second, that both inside and outside the fence there were communities equally involved in this process.

This example is offered simply to describe how material culture and monuments from the recent past are necessary for a full interpretation of the Cold War, told through its material culture as opposed to the highly politicised oral accounts of participants; many documentary sources for this period are unlikely to become available for some time, and media accounts again will be biased and politically spun. Archaeological meth-

Fig. 3.3. Stone circle at Peace Camp, Nevada.

ods and theory provide the conditions for description and interpretation, and remembering even this most recent of times.

Decisions to preserve sites largely for reasons of interpretation are generally well-meaning and will often be successful, given the level of public interest in this recent period of history. But how the past is interpreted will also have significance, as Uzzell has explained (1994, 1999) in justifying a 'hot' approach to interpretation. Numerous examples are cited in Schofield (1999, in press) of the manner of interpretation and the eloquence of monuments and buildings, art and objects in conveying the character of modern warfare.

We have already discussed conservation along the Western Front. It is well known that some places survive as sacred landscapes, virtually unaltered since their abandonment in 1918, while others on the front line are littered with memorials and graves. Yet others are almost relict cultural landscapes in the sense of earthwork remains of trench systems, concrete emplacements and tunnels left to natural decay and not subject to human intervention. Finally some places have seen reconstruction, forcing the contemporary scene upon visitors. The re-excavated and almost manufactured trenches at Vimy Ridge are an example of this. But it is places where all forms of interpretive display are available that contribute most to the visitors' experience of the Front: here there is time depth, and food for thought, both relating to the conditions of battle, and conservation management – how can the story be told for all, and the sacredness of the landscape still retained? I want here to make one specific point, and one that relates to a comment by Virilio, about 'playful warring, after the real warring' (1991, 15). Children engage with the past in very different ways from adults, and a key approach is through play. This is often frowned upon, especially at sacred sites. However, there should be nothing wrong with play. Military sites should have the capacity to serve as playgrounds in the same way as military museums provide tanks as climbing frames. Children learn through play, and opportunities for play will be a valuable addition to many military sites.

As a critique on contemporary life

A motivation frequently cited for undertaking archaeologies of the modern period, the contemporary past, is to provide a new dimension, a critique on modern life. As Graves Brown has written:

> the key is to accept that we are ourselves part of the world we seek to understand and, rather than seeking to stand aside from society and pontificate upon it, we need to be within the process and, albeit critically, allow experience to guide our understanding (2000, 7).

This is true for all studies of modern material culture, not least the legacy of militarisation. We can use archaeology to assess our own society's willingness to take up arms, to form alliances and co-operate within broader strategic objectives. We can assess the validity and accuracy of received wisdom, and question the motivations for presenting information about military operations as fact. What were we not told, and why? And we can use archaeology to question the distinctions that exist between what we are told, and what actually happened. Artefacts recovered from excavations of recent sites may give some insight, as might their spatial distribution.

The degree to which archaeology allows us to deconstruct places and episodes with which we have close familiarity has yet to be fully explored (see Schofield 2004 for some ideas of how this might contribute); but the potential is obvious and achievable if set within the context of well-thought-out research agenda.

Crime and retribution

Although not wishing to dwell on this as a motivation, it does have relevance and is significant in some cases. In Cambodia, for example, Helen Jarvis (2002) has recently described the attempts to provide a sound basis for bringing the Khmer Rouge to justice for war crimes and atrocities during the Kampuchea period of 1975-9. She outlines how the Cambodian Genocide Programme and the Documentation Center of Cambodia has accumulated a wealth of data – much reliant upon archaeological evidence – to reveal the 'massive and systematic nationwide scope of the Khmer Rouge's human rights violations' (2002, 92). Similarly in Argentina, where Crossland (2002) describes the work of the Argentinian Forensic Anthropology Team, responsible for excavating the unmarked graves of people who were 'disappeared' during the military dictatorship of 1976-83.

3. *Memory and meaning*

A final example also comes from Argentina: the Club Athletico in Buenos Aires, described by Dolff-Bonekaemper as,

> a clandestine detention center built in 1977 by the military government into the cellar of a former warehouse. ...
> The detention center's plan shows a row of cells, measuring 1.5 meters by 1.5 meters, with some larger rooms at one end of the building (2002b, 9).

This is one of many centres around the country where people were detained, having been suspected of subversive actions or beliefs. Prisoners were questioned and often tortured and killed. The bodies of the 'disappeared' were frequently thrown into the river. After a brief period of use the Club was obscured by the construction of a highway.

There is now a memorial park in Buenos Aires dedicated to the memory of the disappeared, yet despite this, sites like the Club Atletico provide a more tangible link to those detained there. In 2002 excavation was begun, revealing walls and floors, and the prisoners' graffiti, with the aim of finding out as much as possible. People in the neighbourhood were interviewed to elaborate on the material recovered by excavation. 'The aim is to connect memory and places and to establish a topography of events based on individual topographies of memory' (Dolff-Bonekaemper 2002b, 10).

Sense of place

Sense of place involves the aura and atmosphere of a place, the states of mind among those most affected by it, and the sense of inhabitation that often characterises places of conflict. The first two of these are perhaps the easiest to define as they relate quite simply to experience and ownership of place.

A place will have particular characteristics that set it apart often from all others but certainly from those which surround and define it (Fairclough 2003). People's experience of that place will relate directly to those characteristics, either in the sense of borrowing from them or constructing them in the first place. Let me give an example. Along the Western Front are a diversity of battlefield landscapes that have been either conserved or abandoned, or returned to agriculture. Unless there is some personal connection with those remains buried in a field now under cultivation, this last situation is unlikely to generate any real sense of past or place. A conserved or reconstructed set of trenches is equally unlikely to provoke significant emotional response, except perhaps in providing a directly visual sense of what it was like to pass along a trench, or the view afforded 'over the top'. In the case of abandoned landscapes, with their earthworks and regenerated woodland in the danger-zones where unexploded ordnance often prevents visitor access, however, a sense of authenticity and of existence and use will be felt by many visitors (though the contradiction is unfortunate: those places least conducive to conveying sense of place are the most accessible). What precisely provokes this sense is largely based on individual experience and knowledge of the place and its history, and as such defies definition. But for me, a quiet and empty landscape that once rattled to the sound of artillery; a peaceful landscape that once saw death; and a cultural landscape which retains physical traces that link the past with the present are the necessary conditions for sensing sites of conflict in an intimate and engaging way.

On this matter I take issue with Laurent Olivier, who states that we would like to think that these sites intrinsically preserve the memory of events, where they have been the scenes of tragedy. He goes on:

In fact, neither places nor things say anything whatsoever in themselves, unless it is to those who have memories of them. 'The countryside, there, for you is empty, says Pierre Nivromort to his grandchildren during his return to Auschwitz, but for me it is full of people: here I see women in rags digging a trench; I can smell burnt flesh' (interview in *Liberation*, 3 October 1996). What do we do when faced with these sites that are empty of meaning? To become witness to this incommunicable past, it becomes necessary to tell stories; that is, to invent a story that could be told by the remains, or by the traces of past events. This is, essentially, the museum's role (2001, 184).

I take issue for two reasons: first, because I don't believe that places say nothing in themselves. Maybe this is a personal thing, but like Bell (1997) I experience places, whether I have known them or not. It is hard to describe what that feeling is, and what it represents, but there is something that communicates to me a sense of past events; not always, but sometimes and in some places. Secondly, because telling stories certainly need not involve inventing something. Gilbert demonstrated this most eloquently in his (1998) *Holocaust Journey*, in which students were taken to Holocaust sites, at which he read first-hand accounts to them. The impact was extraordinary. Some of the students couldn't take it and returned home. I do agree though that invented stories can magnify the impact of place.

In covering this topic in relation to military action, it is hard to avoid mentioning the 'ghosts of place', described by Bell (1997) as a significant subject in defining and understanding how sense of place is constructed and used. In Scates' (2002) study of pilgrimage to the battlegrounds of Gallipoli, one or two recollections cover the question of ghosts. Now, Bell never meant his theoretical study to be interpreted literally, being far more to do with aura than personal rehabitation from the past. But sites of death and suffering have often been coincident with compelling accounts of rehabitation and presence. The degree of spirituality that accompanied interpretation of First World War battlefields in the immediate aftermath of the War was significant. Winter (1995), for example, describes and shows some of the 'spirit photographs' that depict extra-terrestrial presentations on Armistice Day. Royal Air Force (RAF) stations in World War II are also commonly associated with ghost stories that often defy contradiction, and represent an uneasy linkage between material culture and past lives and social actions. Remembering Bell's (1997) fears of seeming unscientific, I shall repeat just one such instance, from Flanders (after Scates 2002, 17) to illustrate this dimension to discussions of place and rehabilation:

Myra: It happened years ago now when I was still living in England. I was visiting France and a friend of mine asked me to visit her father's grave. ... It was in a little graveyard not one of the large cemeteries. I arrived there and it was ever so cold. ... Well, there were not that many graves but I knew it would take a time to find him and just as I was searching a man came up to me. He said, 'Are you looking for Captain Dove?' I said, 'Well, yes, I am', and he said he would take me to him and he led me straight to the grave. He was very helpful. I asked him how he knew Captain Dove and he said he had served as his batman during the war and of course he was still in uniform. I didn't think anything of that.
Scates: In uniform?
Myra: Yes, in uniform. Well, it was only when I returned home that I thought anything of that. I went to see my friend to let her know I had found her father's grave. I described it for her and I told her about my meeting up with his batman. She stopped then and looked me straight in the eye. 'But Myra', she said, 'My father and his batman were both killed together.'

3. Memory and meaning

Cultural identity and ideology

The cultural landscape, and the places within it, are constantly changing, rarely more so than at times of war or in its aftermath. We can see this for the Cold War, and how its closure in 1989 led to rapid assimilation in the former East of Western cultural traditions. We can also see this at landscape scale, Szpanowski (2002) noting, for example, how in Poland the decline of intensive agriculture and the rise of new farming strategies provided opportunities for improved systems and policies aimed at the sustained protection of the cultural landscape. The Polish countryside is also 'burdened by the legacy of the state farms, which collapsed simultaneously with the communist and socialist systems' (ibid., 128). The result of this was thousands of acres of wasteland, thousands of unemployed people and over 2,000 historic manor houses awaiting new ownership and conservation.

Albania has also seen significant change in recent years. In exploring how material culture is used as an indicator of change, Galaty et al. (1999) have examined Communist era bunkers (their term, but translated from the Albanian *bunkeri*) and second-century AD architectural blocks as the material representations of two competing ideologies: domination and resistance. The authors use this material culture specifically to 'stimulate archaeological thinking about the formulation and manipulation of landscapes and the interplay between domination and resistance as an agent of change' (ibid., 197).

Albania presented something of a mystery to outsiders during the Communist era. Visitors, however, frequently reported their observations, and the proliferation of *bunkeri* was one of these. Within the authors' survey area these structures were seen almost literally everywhere. Through the Cold War Albania was initially allied with Russia and later China, but in the later 1970s it split with all its Communist allies, and the *bunkeri* were a feature of this isolationist policy, designed as a last ditch defence against foreign invasion. In all, from 1967 to 1986 400,000 to 800,000 concrete bunkers – each reinforced with thirteen layers of steel – were constructed, one for every four to five Albanians. This was domination psychology *in extremis*, even to the point that the maintenance of bunkers was the responsibility of individual families, thereby 'binding local communities into an infrastructure of authority extending all the way to the centre, in Tirana' (ibid., 203). In retrospect it is hardly surprising that most Albanians regard these bunkers as little more than symbols of intimidation and control. They now have new meaning, being ignored and even ridiculed. Some have been removed, primarily in urban areas where heavy lifting equipment is available; however most remain either as abandoned structures or re-used as sheepfolds, kennels and so on.

But the interpretation of militarised zones and landscape can extend beyond the obvious and monumental, to more subtle traces reflecting the treatment of other cultural remains. Also in Albania is evidence that the dominant Communist regime sought to destroy all trace of dissident ideologies. As was the case in China during the 1960s and 70s, for example, local Communist parties razed and destroyed 2,169 churches and mosques (Rugg 1994). There is also evidence that archaeological material, in this case a second-century AD architectural block, was being taken from ancient sites reconstructed under the Communist regime to signify domination and placed at the churches seemingly to fulfil a role in their rebuilding. Galaty et al. interpret this as evidence of resistance that seems hard to dispute.

What this example shows is the degree to which material culture can be both manipulated and created by the dominant regime, and then re-used and re-appropriated in its aftermath. The cultural landscape is ever-changing and the role of monuments, places and objects in interpretation will be both flexible and diverse as a result.

3. Memory and meaning

Discord value and enabling a debate

There are some instances where archaeological investigation provokes debate and interest in some forgotten past; something that society is not proud of, and which has gone largely unrecorded and unacknowledged for some time. This has been termed 'dissonant heritage' (Tunbridge and Ashworth 1999), 'heritage that hurts' (Uzzell 1998) and perhaps most appropriately here, heritage with 'discord value'. This term has been used by Dolff-Bonekaemper (nd) to mean, among other things, the provocation of 'strong opinions and discord, encouraging debates which had not taken place before for want of a suitable venue' (ibid., 57). As the author goes on to explain,

> [This] would encourage the conservation of pointers to recent history such as the Berlin Wall, traces of the Iron Curtain or other remnants of dictatorships or civil conflict. Such objects are often a source of fierce argument and in danger of disappearing before the controversy for which they may well provide a venue dies down. At a later stage, the 'discord value' will probably turn into historical value, serving as justification for lasting conservation (ibid., 57).

The Neue Wache in Berlin is an example that Dolff-Bonekaemper uses to illustrate the value of this criterion. In 1993 Chancellor Kohl decided to use Neue Wache, built in 1816-18 on the Unter den Linden in Berlin, as a site for a memorial to the victims of war and tyranny. However, this took little account of the building's original use to commemorate the victory of Prussian troops over Napoleon's army in 1814-15. As Dolff-Bonekaemper puts it:

> The new use of the building by the federal state, the victor

in the German unification process, resurrected its semantics: the iconography of victory assumed importance once
again, becoming a bone of contention (ibid., 55).

Under these conditions would it be permissible to return
monuments commemorating victorious generals to their original location next to the building, or did the new function of the
building rule that out? Thus Neue Wache became a site of
discord, the place provoking debate on the state of Germany
four years after the Wall, on similarities and differences in the
collective cultural memory of West and East Germans, and
finally on Prussian history (ibid.).

This degree of politicised debate and deliberation has also
been the case with Makronisos, a small uninhabited island off
Greece's Attica coast where the most notorious of concentration
camps was established by the Greek government during the
Civil War (1946-9). As Hamilakis states,

[this] was a place of brutality, torture and death, but its
distinctive feature was its role as an indoctrination center
for many thousands of political dissidents ... who, after
they were 're-educated' in the national dogmas, were sent
to fight against their ex-comrades (2002, 307).

Antiquity provided clear focus for constructing among these
dissidents national time, national memories and − paradoxi-
cally − counter-memories. It is of interest here that despite the
'difficulty' felt in dealing with Makronisos, it was nevertheless
recognised as a 'historical site' and 'locus of memory' by Minis-
terial decree in 1989. Its buildings were deemed worthy of
preservation and a number have now been restored. Reunions
are now held on the island, and there are demands that all state
archives become available. Makronisos is now becoming 'part of
the national memory in the name of a de-politicized "national

reconciliation" ', despite the resistance of some former inmates (ibid, 329).

Finally, there is Landzelius's study of Swedish labour-company camps, established by the military in the 1930s. Two types of camp were constructed: one, of which eight examples were built across Sweden, was for those on the political left and labelled as Communists; the other comprised a single camp to contain 'undiscliplined elements'. Landzelius's conclusions relate closely to what we refer to here as motivations of not forgetting, while also causing us to confront the past. Landzelius proposed that:

> Objects of the past ... should be mobilised as disinheritance for critical and subversive purposes in order to make the past implode into the present in ways that unsettle fundamental social imaginary significations.

He goes on, provocatively, to suggest that,

> one such disinheritance assemblage, in the form of a reconstructed [labour-company] camp, [could, or should?] be erected in the courtyard of the Royal Palace in Stockholm, where the Nazi sympathizer King Gustav V resided during the war. In this way the marginalized past would be critically relocated to the centre, and the silencing authority behind the exhortation 'a Swede keeps quiet' would be crucially decentered. ... such disinheritance assemblages could, as part of a politico-spatial struggle for the advancement of democratic principles and accountability, be made into 'touring exhibitions' resituated into centres of power and abjection. The very fact that the provocative appearance of disinheritance assemblages would most probably lead to discontent and conflicts indicates the importance of making issues of memorialisation

the objective of open and public political deliberation (2003, 216).

Summary

This chapter has attempted to cover some of the middle ground between identifying what constitutes military heritage, and the archaeological approach that can be adopted for studying it, and how that resource should then be managed to best effect. This middle ground has included the justifications for military heritage: why it matters and to whom. In attempting to separate out some of these motivations and constituencies, divisions and partition have been introduced where perhaps they do not exist. There is certainly much overlap here, and in that sense the headings may be misleading. But they do enable us to focus on some of the main criteria, and examples of their particular relevance.

I shall now move on to the next stage in what is commonly referred to as the management cycle: how the places identified as having value should be managed, and what options exist for doing so.

4

Managing matériel culture

The structure of this book conforms to the process by which material culture is first understood, documented and contextualised (Chapter 2), given meaning and significance (Chapter 3), then protected or at least taken account of where threatened, for example with development (this chapter). Finally – in some cases only – this material culture is interpreted and presented, enjoyed and visited (Chapter 5).

This chapter therefore covers significant ground, but ground defined by the conservation practices of nations and political authorities. While the philosophies that dictate approaches to and perceptions of military heritage can be Europe-wide or even global, the application of those philosophies will be defined within administrative and political boundaries. Here I will focus on the approach taken to recent military remains in England, though making reference to approaches elsewhere. The chapter also serves as a case study in how to afford protection to these sites of conflict. How do we choose which sites are significant (ground covered partly in the previous chapter), and what mechanisms exist for protecting them? The chapter is written at a time when heritage legislation in England is under review. It nevertheless remains an example of best practice, albeit within the constraints of a draconian and rather fragmented system, and one in a state of flux.

The chapter will first outline the main points of the current system for managing cultural resources in England; it will then describe the criteria by which sites are assessed as having 'national importance' or 'special interest', but outlining also an approach that recognises meaning and value in all places, not just those that are traditionally considered 'special'; I will then outline some of the main protective regimes and how they are applied to military sites in England, though with occasional examples from elsewhere to set England's approach in its wider context.

Heritage management in England

I should begin by stating how little I like the term 'heritage'. It implies something exclusive and privileged. Certainly in most dictionary definitions this is true: it suggests something special and noteworthy, and something that is inherited. First, we should begin by recognising all material culture as special; we have already seen how places and objects can mean different things to different people – the social significance considerations that Byrne et al. (2001) describe take this principle as a starting point. Put simply, everywhere will have meaning and significance to somebody, and to produce a list of special places immediately relegates those sites not on the list – at least in the eyes of some – to having no value at all. Secondly, I have concerns over the idea that heritage is inherited. To take Graves Brown's point (2000, 7 and above), we don't stand aside from society and pontificate upon it; we are part of the world we seek to understand. We therefore contribute to it; we create and manipulate. We reconfigure our own material world – we don't just inherit it.

One can take this further. I am reminded of the debate a short time ago about the past being a non-renewable resource, again implying that we have simply inherited something from a time past. As Holtorf (2002) so eloquently explained, this simply isn't so – we know what the argument means in its literal sense (that once an archaeological site has been destroyed it has gone forever); but what I refer to here is the archaeological resource as whole, which is renewable. It is constantly being added to, altered and having things removed. It is transient. Today's archaeological resource is very different to that of fifty years ago (much of our landscape is now late twentieth-century in character), and the resource even in ten years time will be significantly different again. One of the greatest impacts upon that archaeological resource was during World War II. Many archaeological sites were destroyed by airfield construction, and as a result of bomb damage. But renewal (not replacement – no one questions that specific archaeological resources are irreplaceable) came in the form of, for example, airfields built on the sites of Roman villas and medieval settlements; pillboxes dug into the centres of round barrows; and many other newly constructed sites which together comprise a significant and substantial new layer to the cultural landscape map. I once suggested that World War II added one million sites to the UK's archaeological resources. Once all of the various – and often very ephemeral – anti-invasion defences are added up, and the air raid shelters, and airfields and anti-aircraft gunsites and so on, the figure may not be far short of that.

All of this has direct relevance to us as archaeologists: it is this material culture, whether ancient or modern, that we apply our archaeological minds and methods to investigating and interpreting. So not heritage perhaps, but an archaeological resource, as Bill Bryson once commendably described it (1996, 103-4).

Notwithstanding reservations over the terminology we are required to use – and which has its advantages: people do understand, or think they understand, what heritage is – there is a system in place which enables those employed with national heritage agencies, local authorities and others, to manage this resource within a fairly robust and effective systemic framework (Figure 4.1). English Heritage holds much of the responsibility for this. Set up under the terms of the 1983 National Heritage Act, its role is to advise the British government on cultural heritage matters in England: such as the protection of sites and their subsequent management. English Heritage holds in 'guardianship' over 600 properties, all of which are publicly accessible. Some of these have a recent military component, such as at Tilbury Fort (Essex) and Dover Castle and Dover Western Heights (Kent). English Heritage also commissions projects that together contribute to new thinking on archaeological and cultural heritage matters, and sets standards for scientific endeavour and analysis, buildings recording and so on.

Separately from English Heritage, various government departments also contribute at this national strategic level. In 1990, for example, the then Department of the Environment produced Planning Policy Guidance Note 16: Archaeology and Planning (PPG16, DoE 1990) which established archaeological remains as a material matter within the planning system, and the presumption that nationally important remains should be preserved in situ, whether legally protected or not. Much archaeological work has since been commissioned using the 'polluter pays' principle established under this government guidance.

Heritage management also operates at local level, through local and unitary authorities. Their role includes the implementation of PPG16 through the detailed assessment of individual planning applications, but also more proactively through the drafting of structure and local plans, which include policies for archaeology and cultural heritage within the area covered by the plan. A local plan policy may, for example, make specific reference to an area having a character determined largely by its former use as a military site, and stating that development proposals must take that character into account. Local authori-

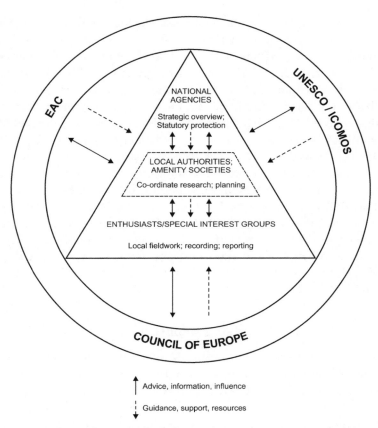

Fig. 4.1. Management frameworks for cultural heritage matters in England.

ties will often also produce literature for public distribution. Somerset County Council, for instance, has produced a leaflet describing military sites in the county.

Although nominally at the bottom of the pyramid, it is the wide base that accommodates important contributors in the form of local communities and enthusiast groups (Figure 4.1). There are many of these and, as we have seen in previous chapters, strong local attachment is felt towards military structures, especially it would seem from World War II. Campaigns (sometimes co-ordinated through the Council for British Archaeology) and information about forthcoming developments often work up from this level, through the local authority to English Heritage and the government department who will ultimately decide whether some form of statutory protection is appropriate. It is also at this local level that much valuable fieldwork is conducted; the Heritage Lottery Funded Defence of Britain Project, and the work that preceded it, are examples.

Finally, there is the international context within which all of this sits. The International Council on Monuments and Sites (ICOMOS) has influence here, as does the Council of Europe (e.g. Dolff-Bonekaemper 2004), and within the aegis of the latter the EAC – European Archaeological Colloquium, effectively a meeting of the state heritage agencies of Europe. It is within these related contexts that work on military heritage is conducted in the UK.

Judging importance

Decisions to retain some military sites, or objects, or components of landscape, are generally taken on the basis of their relative significance. For a site to be considered for scheduling as a monument, for example (see below for more on this) it must be demonstrably of 'national importance'; to qualify for listing buildings must display some combination of architectural or historic interest, close historical association or group value. In the past – and specifically under English Heritage's Monuments Protection Programme or MPP (Startin 1993; English Heritage 2000) – this evaluation was rigorously applied through a system of numerical calculation, supported by the professional judgement of informed observers. Now emphasis is placed far more on professional judgement and especially so for the modern period. I will illustrate how this works by using the

example of the United States Air Force base at Greenham
Common (West Berkshire) and the decision-making process
which led to that site being recognised by English Heritage as
having national importance and eventually becoming in part a
scheduled monument.

Greenham Common and the Cold War

Greenham Common airbase was included – alongside other
sites – in a national assessment of England's Cold War resources undertaken by English Heritage (Cocroft 2001). Following an overview of Cold War sites, involving detailed field
survey by archaeologists of the then Royal Commission on the
Historical Monuments of England (RCHME), and subsequently
published (Cocroft and Thomas 2003), this assessment of Cold
War sites was based on significance criteria developed partly
through the experience of earlier work, but also set within the
context of the non-statutory criteria outlined in PPG16,
namely:

> Period
> Rarity
> Documentation
> Group value
> Survival/condition
> Fragility/vulnerability
> Diversity
> Potential
> > (DoE 1990, Annex 4).

The report (Cocroft 2001) set out the historical context of
Britain's experience of the Cold War, within the framework of
its significant role within the North Atlantic Treaty Organisation (NATO). During this period the Cold War provided the

background to all spheres of public life: political, economic, scientific and cultural. Two main phases of the Cold War were identified, providing further context for interpreting and 'judging' its field remains: the First Cold War (1945-62) with a massive rearmament and building programme in the period 1950-62, and the Second Cold War (1980-89) with its hardening programme for established bases. Between the two was a period of sustained deterrence with a major building programme, especially in the late 1970s.

The second stage was to refine the non-statutory criteria to serve the needs of this very recent cultural resource. The criteria worked well for earlier field remains, but had shortcomings when it came to assessing massively monumental and very recent remains, where technology and associations over long distances were more significant than for earlier sites and structures. Furthermore there were complications over attributing historical significance to sites that were so recent. For World War II sites historic importance is often easy to determine: clear events and battles that determined the course of the war. But for the Cold War this was less clear-cut. What set this era apart was the degree to which the UK became involved in post-war political alliances and changing political strategy. Technological developments accelerated to the extent that 'new' technology was often replaced before its impact could be felt. The development of nuclear technology and its potential impact on society was a major concern at this time, and especially during the Second Cold War. Thus structures and places designed to develop, test, assemble and handle nuclear weapons, and to operate them within a post-nuclear attack environment were considered the most distinctive and characteristic monuments of the period. The full set of criteria developed for assessing Cold War monuments in England is set out in Table 4.1 (see also Cocroft, in press).

4. Managing matériel culture

Survival/condition

1   Structural integrity and survival of original internal configuration, plant and fittings.

2   Re-use for another purpose. Time depth may add historic value to a structure.

3   Survival of contemporary setting, character, spatial relationships – group value in other words. An important component contributing to the character of these sites might be tree planting, which is found at some radar stations and missile sites.

Period

4   Representative of a particular phase of the Cold War. An example is the early 1950s anti-aircraft sites designed to counter attacks by manned piston-engined aircraft, but these were obsolete within a few years as jet aircraft and unmanned missiles emerged as the main threat.

5   Centrality to British/NATO defence policy. Features and structures associated with the British V-force for example, which was central to British nuclear deterrent policy from the late 1950s to the 1960s, or NATO cruise missiles during the 1980s.

6   Technological significance. As well as being Cold War structures, many sites are important monuments to post-war British achievements in science and technology.

Rarity

7   In nearly all cases individual monument types are rare. Many of the structures carried out unique functions, so are rare almost by definition. While rarity and uniqueness are criteria for protection, they will be supported by other usually technological reasons.

Diversity

8   Some site types exhibit a number of different structural forms, although designed to fulfil a similar function.

Cultural and amenity value

9   Sites will often be suited to a combination of education, understanding, tourism and public access.

Table 4.1. Criteria for assessing Cold War monuments (after Cocroft 2001).

A third stage in this evaluative process was to produce a typology of Cold War monument classes, again based on field survey (Cocroft and Thomas 2003). This resulted in nine categories being defined, which divide into thirty-one monument classes, within most of which is a diversity of distinctive types (Table 4.2). One of the categories was United States Air Force, and within that the monument class Cruise missile sites. A statement of importance noted:

> Cruise missile sites, through their Europe-wide distribution, testify to the resolve of the principal partners in NATO to maintain nuclear parity with the countries of the Warsaw Pact. They also represent examples of leading edge technological innovation which characterised the western post-war defence industry. ... Six cruise missile sites were constructed in Europe during the mid-1980s, two in England, and single bases in Belgium, Germany, the Netherlands and Italy. The two bases in England are at RAF Molesworth (Cambridgeshire) and Greenham Common (Berkshire); both survive intact (Cocroft 2001).

The Ground-launched cruise missiles Alert and Maintenance Area (GAMA) at Greenham was therefore of national importance, and was selected for protection. The statement of significance provided the full justification for retaining this particular monument:

> The GAMA complex was one of only six built in Europe ... it has the distinction of being the longest commissioned of the group. Structurally the complex remains intact, its massive architecture reflecting NATO's financial commitment to this system, and its centrality in contemporary NATO strategy. Its design asserts an ability to survive a Soviet conventional pre-emptive strike and still launch a retaliatory attack.
>
> Included within [the GAMA site] is a group of early 1950s bombstores or igloos. These were used by the cruise missile wing , but are also illustrative of the earlier phase of Cold War activity on the airfield.
>
> The international importance of the GAMA site is as

4. Managing matériel culture

Categories	Monument classes
Air Defence	Radar Royal Observer Corps Anti-aircraft guns Surface to air missiles Fighter interceptor airfields
Nuclear Deterrent	V-bomber airfields Nuclear weapons stores Thor missile sites
United States Air Force	Airfields Cruise missile sites
Defence Research Establishments	Aviation Naval Rockets, guided weapons Nuclear Miscellaneous
Defence manufacturing sites	Defence manufacturing sites
Emergency Civil Government	Early 1950s War Rooms Regional Seats of Government Sub Regional Headquarters Regional Government Headquarters Local Authority Emergency Headquarters Civil Defence structures The utilities Private nuclear shelters
Emergency Provisions Stores	Grain silos Cold stores General purpose stores Fuel depots
Communications	Underground telephone exchanges Microwave tower network
Miscellaneous	The peace movement

Table 4.2. Typology for Cold War monuments (after Cocroft 2001).

one of the key emblematic monuments of the 'Second Cold War', signifying an escalation of the nuclear arms race by the introduction of ground launched cruise missiles [GLCM] during the early 1980s, potentially providing NATO with a first strike capability. Subsequent to the INF Treaty most of the missiles and launchers were destroyed: GAMA remains as one of the few tangible relics of this technology. Its derelict condition remains a potent symbol of the positive power of arms control treaties to render advanced military technology obsolete.

Beyond its significance as an exemplar of the infrastructure of GLCM technology the GAMA complex had a wider significance in the late twentieth century as the centre of mass protest, especially by women's groups, against the nuclear arms race.

The value of the USAF site is enhanced by surviving archive material held on-site, detailed unit histories preserved in the United States, and the potential for these to be supplemented by oral testimony. Complimentary archive sources also exist relating to the women's peace camp (Cocroft 2001).

The approach here therefore involved establishing bespoke criteria which related closely to those non-statutory criteria with which heritage managers and others were closely familiar, but which were more effective for remains that are both robust and recent in date. A contextual framework was also established for monuments of the Cold War period, giving them chronological reference, and setting them within their political and social contexts. A typology was defined, and the criteria applied to examples of each Monument Class (or each Monument Type where these were established). This resulted in a list of sites (detailed in Cocroft 2001) deemed to have national importance. How then to manage those sites, and what protective measures may be appropriate for them will be discussed below.

First, it is worth citing one other example here, to highlight the similarity of approach taken to a diversity of remains.

Crashed military aircraft

Although the type of site is very different, the approach is similar, first determining so far as possible an original population, and second, establishing the number of crashed aircraft alongside modern survivals (in museums and private collections for instance) and within a chronological context. Some of the following will sound familiar. English Heritage (2002, 6) state that they recognise:

> [the] importance of [military aircraft crash] sites in terms of survival, rarity or historic importance, and would wish to minimize unnecessary disturbance to examples that meet a combination of the following criteria:
>
> (1) The crash site includes components of an aircraft of which very few or no known complete examples survive. Examples of the commonplace may also be considered of importance where they survive well and meet one or more of the other criteria.
> (2) The remains are well preserved, and may include key components such as engines, fuselage sections, main planes, undercarriage units and gun turrets. Those crash sites for which individual airframe identities (serial numbers) have been established will be of particular interest.
> (3) The aircraft was associated with significant raids, campaigns or notable individuals.
> (4) There is potential for display or interpretation as historic features within the landscape (for example as

127

upland crash site memorials), or for restoration and display of the crashed aircraft as a rare example of its type.

Crash sites can be scheduled, where the criteria are met and where this designation is considered appropriate. This will rarely happen, however. In most cases these nationally important crash sites will more likely be subject to tighter controls where excavation or recording is proposed. One of the key points of English Heritage's guidance on this subject concerned the need for fully developed project designs for crash site excavations, including method statements, as well as proposals for the recovery, conservation and storage of artefacts, archiving and publication.

Protective regimes and the management of change

Characterisation and context

Before addressing the management choices that apply to particular sites I will return briefly to characterisation (Fairclough and Rippon 2002; Fairclough 2003). This is an approach to managing change within the historic and contemporary environments that begins by taking a holistic view as opposed to focusing on special places, and concerns relevance and context, not significance. Characterisation tends to work best at the higher levels of strategic and spatial planning, the products being maps with relational databases, usually on Geographical Information Systems held within local authorities, identifying the distinctive characteristics of the modern landscape but showing the influence of earlier activity on its present form. So character areas may relate to the continued presence of earlier field patterns, or residential areas in a town that reflect earlier origins. Characterisation can also highlight industrialised landscapes, such as those characteristic of tin mining in Cornwall, and it can demonstrate the influence of militarisation, in the form of airfields and army camps for instance. The point here is that this approach is more concerned with landscape scale; it doesn't pick up the detail.

I refer to characterisation here as it gives context to understanding the role of other more site-orientated protection and management regimes. For example, while scheduling will provide protection for a control tower on an airfield, characterisation can ensure that planning decisions which may determine the future use of an abandoned airfield take the form of that airfield, its characteristics, its legacy and its impact on the surrounding landscapes and community into account. Airfields can be scheduled in their entirety (they are 'buildings, structures or works' in the terms of the Ancient Monuments and Archaeological Areas Act, 1979), but as we will see that rather assumes that the entire site will then remain as a monument, out of everyday use. For a site as extensive and with as much potential for brownfield redevelopment as an airfield, in a place as crowded as the UK, that seems unlikely to be a realistic or sustainable option. And if a scheduled airfield is to be redeveloped, even in part, then the point of scheduling the entire site is lost. These are issues we can now discuss in more detail.

The main options available for the protection of heritage places in England, whether archaeological sites, specific areas of landscape or parkland, or buildings, divide into statutory and non-statutory. Statutory measures include scheduling, listing and conservation areas; non-statutory means include registers (the compilation of which had statutory backing, but there are no statutory controls relating to sites entered on the Register), protection through various agri-environment schemes, and management of change through planning conditions imposed through the development control process. Also non-statutory are World Heritage Sites. That said, I prefer to use outcomes as the basis for the following discussion. They are: in situ preservation; adaptive re-use; symbolic representation; and recording, recognising that several of these options may have relevance on a single site. Underlying all of this is the canvas provided by characterisation, which will contribute to these discussions at a higher strategic level (what was previously called structure or strategic planning, now more commonly referred to as spatial planning), and the need for sustainable solutions. Also important is the principle of informed conservation (Clark 2001): taking decisions on the basis of knowledge and understanding; decisions taken in ignorance will more often than not be bad decisions.

In situ preservation

This tends to be the decision taken when society cannot afford to lose the site or building in question: in other words where it is a critical asset (in sustainable development parlance, see English Heritage 1997). These will invariably be sites of national importance or special interest which English Heritage or local authorities, and sometimes private trusts, decide meet the various criteria for statutory protection, or have significant local or community-based interest or value. But beyond deciding to retain a monument or building in situ, one must also decide what future use is deemed both appropriate and likely given its location, the state and condition of the place, and the approach and attitude of its current or prospective owners. One option is to retain buildings in use, or to find some new use (the subject of the next section). This inevitably brings some change of character, though the benefits of that, in meeting social and economic needs, for example, may outweigh other conservation interests. Re-use may also extend the life of the building. After all, abandoned buildings will generally (and quickly) become monuments.

But here our concern is for those structures which we wish to retain as they are, as monuments or ruined buildings, or crashed aircraft that should remain untouched, as sacred and buried sites. How can these places be effectively managed and protected?

Perhaps the best known approach is to protect them through designation as a scheduled monument (note I have deliberately dropped the 'ancient' from this phrase), under the terms of the 1979 Ancient Monuments and Archaeological Areas Act. Scheduling as a designation has a history dating back to 1882, when the first sites (all prehistoric and monumental) were added to the list or 'Schedule'. The implications of scheduling have changed somewhat since then. It is now quite a severe form of designation, quite draconian and potentially restricting. It is important to note two things here. First, that the decision to add a monument to the Schedule is taken by the Secretary of State, currently in the Department for Culture, Media and Sport, on advice generally from English Heritage; but this is a decision on which the Secretary of State can exercise discretion: the Secretary of State *may* recommend scheduling any monument of national importance. Scheduling will generally be recommended only where the designation is appropriate, and where it is felt either necessary or to be of benefit to the monument in question. Second, that scheduling itself is not the constraint. Once scheduled the owner must apply for prior Scheduled Monument Consent (SMC) for any works that involve damaging, removing, altering or destroying any part of a monument, or flooding or tipping on it. It is the refusal of consent (if that is the response) that acts as a constraint. In reality consent is rarely refused outright, and only where proposals are likely to damage significant archaeological remains. More often a compromise is found. Where the owner is granted consent, and where archaeological damage will occur, or where archaeological remains are thought likely, some excavation or recording may be required, and the costs for this would normally be borne by the developer or owner – the 'polluter pays' principle, in other words.

The Ground-launched cruise missiles Alert and Maintenance Area (GAMA) at Greenham Common is a scheduled monument and is privately owned. Here scheduling ensures that a nationally important – and hugely iconic – Cold War monument is not subjected to unnecessary damage. Scheduling is no protection against vandalism (unless vandals are caught in the act), but can be used as the basis for discussing potential uses that are both viable and reasonable, and which neither damage the material remains nor compromise the site's visual integrity; its cohesion and legibility. Currently the site is unused, but with six massive shelters, and numerous other buildings at the south-west corner of a former airfield now reverted to common, sustainable new uses are limited. When new uses are proposed English Heritage staff, alongside the local authority (as inevitably here planning permission would also be needed) and commoners, would immediately and necessarily be drawn into the discussions. Suggestions which may be viable within the context of a scheduled monument might include some interpretation centre or museum (Schofield and Anderton 2000), perhaps in combination with light industrial use. Given the recent history of Greenham and the opposition and conflict it generated, perhaps something of local social and economic benefit would be best: re-using the workshops and garages to train young offenders in vehicle maintenance, for instance.

The former prisoner of war camp at Harperley (County Durham) is also now a scheduled monument. Although it is only one of several former purpose-built prisoner of war camps to survive in England (Thomas 2003), most were not considered for scheduling as the sites were in use as light industrial parks, or were in an advanced state of decay: in neither case would scheduling be appropriate, unless some management regime was agreed which sought to stabilise the processes of erosion and decay or revert these sites to their former appearance, perhaps in the context of a heritage attraction. For a site like this in industrial use the practical implications of scheduling could make it unviable, the owner/occupier of each individual industrial unit having to submit frequent consent applications for the minor works that would enable the business to function. This burden would be unnecessary, inappropriate and deeply unpopular. In the case of Harperley, a heritage attraction is being created, through the willingness and enthusiasm of its owners, an enthusiastic local authority and much publicity generated through the news media and television programmes such as the BBC's *Restoration*. Much of the site remains as an atmospheric reminder of Harperley's wartime past, and a lesson in archaeological conservation, demonstrating to visitors the processes of decay and erosion. The more robust buildings are being restored to serve as the visitor centre and museum. It is hoped that artistic works discovered in the huts, and painted either by German or Italian prisoners kept here, will be restored and redisplayed under improved and stable conditions.

Some pillboxes and coast batteries are also scheduled. In most of these cases their size and form – and sometimes a very remote location – make re-use of any kind unlikely. Here they remain as monuments out of everyday use, but with the legal protection to ensure they are not removed in advance of development or new road schemes, at least not without proper prior consideration.

As we have seen, scheduling is discretionary, and any significant works require prior consent from the Secretary of State, a decision that in England will be based on advice from English Heritage staff. But sites don't have to be scheduled to be recommended for in situ preservation. In situ preservation can also be argued through the planning system (which like heritage legislation is also currently under review). Although advisory, the government-issued Planning Policy Guidance Notes set out the parameters and guidelines to determine how local planning or the newly established unitary authorities deal with planning applications and spatial planning issues. *Planning Policy Guidance Note 16: Archaeology and Planning* (DoE 1990) was crucial in determining the treatment of archaeological sites, noting for example that there should be a presumption that nationally important remains be preserved in situ, whether scheduled or not. PPG16 reinforces the point that scheduling is discretionary and highlights the significance of other options: the decision to accommodate archaeological sites within the context of development proposals, for example, and the possible role of management agreements (something that could become statutory in time, under current designation reform proposals). In practice the future of many military sites is determined through the terms of PPG16, either by placing recording conditions on a development or arguing for in situ preservation.

The presumption in PPG16 that nationally important archaeological remains should be preserved, whether scheduled or not, has had a significant implication for the way archaeological resources are managed. It meant that some archaeological sites that were not 'monuments' in the legal sense could be preserved in situ if they were demonstrably of national importance (prehistoric stone artefact scatters, for example). It also meant that there was less urgency to schedule everything at once: this allowed the national Monuments Protection Programme to be thorough and considered rather than just fast (English Heritage 2000). But most significantly here, it has created a culture in which a more relaxed and consensual approach to management can be taken, for example though the production of management agreements. An example might be a site like RAF Scampton or RAF Wittering, both in Lincolnshire. These airfields were highlighted as significant sites in two separate studies by English Heritage. Scampton was identified as a key World War II site in the Thematic Listing study (Lake 2003), while Wittering was recognised as a key Cold War site

(Cocroft 2001). In the Cold War study the 'H' shaped dispersal pads at Wittering were described as:

> ... a distinctive feature of the ten main airfields developed in the 1950s for Britain's nuclear deterrent V-force. Those at Wittering are good examples of early types without turning loops. Also typical of V-bomber airfields is the circular Compass Swinging Bay attached to one of the 'H' shaped dispersals. ... The group reflects both the massive reordering and investment in the airfield during the mid-1950s and the size, both physically and numerically, of the bombers deployed there. The importance of these features is enhanced by the presence of other contemporary and associated features ... including Operational Readiness Platforms and Loop hardstandings (Cocroft 2001).

Yet both are operational stations, and need to adapt and change perhaps rapidly and radically as the nation's defence needs are reviewed. This is an example of how cultural resource management should work with change rather than against it, and where owners like the Defence Estate are concerned, agreement will often be preferable to designation even though in situ preservation is accepted as the desired outcome.

Military aircraft crash sites qualify for scheduling under the terms of the 1979 Ancient Monuments and Archaeological Areas Act, provided of course they are of national importance. There has been a tendency over the past 20-30 years for some enthusiasts to treat this aspect of aviation heritage as a resource to plunder for financial gain and to build personal collections rather than to consider it a significant archaeological and historic resource (English Heritage 2002; Holyoak 2002; Holyoak and Saunders 2004). One answer to these amateur and sometimes unwelcome interventions would be to schedule crash sites, but that might appear heavy-handed if the aim is

merely to prevent uncontrolled excavation. In fact there is no
desire to stop excavation, merely to ensure that it is properly
thought through, fully justified and well executed and archived,
just as at any other archaeological site. Currently every excavation of a crashed aircraft in the UK requires the excavator to
obtain both the landowner's consent and a licence from the
Personnel Management Agency of the Royal Air Force under
the terms of the 1986 Protection of Military Remains Act.
Licences are currently issued in most cases, except where human remains and/or live ordnance are expected to survive on
board. As was discussed briefly already, English Heritage
(2002) has issued guidance on this matter, suggesting that:
first, historical significance should also be a consideration in
determining applications; and secondly, that any licence application should be accompanied by a fully developed research
design. Provided the system works, scheduling will not be
needed in most cases. The Secretary of State could still use her
discretion, however, and schedule any sites that she felt were
both important and vulnerable, and where excavation – however well thought through – was unlikely to be granted consent.
In line with this, the Personnel Management Agency is currently reviewing its approach to crash sites, and the
circumstances under which licences are issued.

In situ preservation of a rather different kind can be provided by a diversity of agri-environment schemes as well as in
Conservation Areas. Here an opportunity exists to provide a
degree of protection and positive management – perhaps with
financial incentives – to often extensive sites and landscapes.
Government agri-environment schemes came into operation in
England in 1987, since when they have taken an increasingly
active role in the protection and management of the historic
environment (Middleton 2002, 16). In designing these schemes
a balance is typically struck between wildlife, landscape, historic elements, public access, practical approaches to land

management and agricultural factors, meaning that schemes have a broad base with prescriptions that cover a range of circumstances. Examples are the Environmentally Sensitive Areas and Countryside Stewardship schemes (though this too is changing). Under these schemes farmers and landowners can enter voluntary agreements to undertake certain farming practices and capital works to maintain and enhance the rural environment. These can therefore influence the preservation of wartime remains on agricultural land, along the coast, in upland areas, or on extensive sites like former military training areas or airfields.

The same is true of Sites of Special Scientific Interest (SSSI) or Areas of Outstanding Natural Beauty (AONB), where archaeological remains can have protection by default, falling within the boundaries of a protected place on which constraints already exist. In some cases a military presence has aided the preservation of natural environmental resources, qualifying the area for SSSI or AONB status in the first place. This is also often true of National Parks. On Dartmoor, for example, the Okehampton army training area has a degree of protection given its National Park status, irrespective of other designations that exist. Conservation Areas will also apply to military sites, and several airfields have been designated in this way: for example, Biggin Hill (Kent) and Hornchurch (Essex). In these cases it is the preservation of character of the former airfield that is intended, with works that will detract from that character requiring consent from the local planning authority. Conservation Area Appraisals provide a context within which management decisions concerning acceptable change can be determined.

Finally, there are World Heritage sites. Often the emphasis is placed more on how wars and civil unrest threaten the world's heritage resources, and World Heritage Sites in particular. But it is worth remembering the significance of war and conflict in the context of our own cultural history, and especially that of the modern period. For reasons that are hard to determine, there is a reluctance on the part of the World Heritage Convention, administered through UNESCO, to support proposals for military sites to be inscribed on the World Heritage List. Auschwitz, Robben Island and Hiroshima (Beazley in press) are on the World Heritage List, along with numerous earlier fortifications, but nothing more than that. Here is not the place to debate the philosophy behind that approach, whether it be policy or merely preference, but rather to describe briefly what World Heritage Site status means for just one of these places: Robben Island.

First, the criteria by which sites like Robben Island qualified for inscription are worth considering. Proposals to inscribe cultural properties have to meet one or more of six criteria, and for military sites or places of conflict, the following have particular relevance. To qualify sites must:

Cii exhibit an important interchange of human values, over a span of time or within a cultural area of the world, on developments in architecture or technology, monumental arts, town planning, or landscape design;

Ciii bear a unique or at least exceptional testimony to a cultural tradition or to a civilisation which is living or which has disappeared;

Civ be an outstanding example of a type of building or architectural or technological ensemble or landscape which illustrates a significant stage or significant stages in human history;

Cvi be directly or tangibly associated with events or living traditions, with ideas, with beliefs, or with artistic and literary works of outstanding universal significance (a criterion used only in exceptional circumstances, or together with other criteria).

(after Aplin 2002, 165)

4. Managing matériel culture

Robben Island is best known as the prison in which Nelson Mandela and others were held under South Africa's apartheid regime. As Clark says, this is one of the best known cultural heritage sites in the world (2002, 266). Not surprisingly, it met some of the criteria listed above, being inscribed on the World Heritage List in 1999 in recognition of its outstanding universal value to mankind, having previously been designated as a national monument (a comparable status to scheduling). The inscription for Robben Island is based on the significance of the buildings as an 'eloquent testimony to its sombre history', and the fact that 'Robben Island and its prison buildings symbolise the triumph of the human spirit, of freedom, and of democracy over oppression' (cited in Clark 2002, 273-4). Much could be said of this example, though here I will mention just two points (for more information, see Clark 2002): the merits of defining objectives, priorities and change through a management plan; and the importance of the subtle traces in retaining the legacy – the character – of the place.

First, a management plan is encouraged for all sites inscribed on the World Heritage List, and is a requirement for all sites now nominated for inscription. Part of this plan will be a statement of significance, defined in the terms outlined above. Management plans are an important part of cultural heritage management generally, and have a role that extends far beyond the comparatively few World Heritage Sites. The management plan will be based on the principles of informed conservation (Clark 2001), understanding being a necessary prerequisite to informed management decisions. This has been termed CoBRA – Conservation-Based Research and Analysis – defined explicitly as:

The research, analysis, survey and investigation necessary to understand the significance of a building and its

139

landscape, and thus inform decisions about repair, altera-
tion, use and management (ibid., 9).

Management plans contain information about the past and
present uses of the site, what is known about it historically and
archaeologically, the current management regime and how that
could be improved, and what is needed to achieve these aims. It
can be both philosophical (in the sense of what is known, and
what more could be done) and practical (who does what, and
when). The Australian Heritage Commission's *Heritage Places
Workbook* (2001) presents this in an accessible form, listing the
contents of a management plan and defining the distinction
between this and a conservation plan.

For Robben Island the management plan needed to first
understand and document the place as a whole, and as Kate
Clark has written:

> Understanding in this context means having a clear idea
> of what survives today – whether buildings, landscapes,
> archaeology or ecology – and what factors have shaped
> what survives. Understanding, in turn, provides the basis
> for assessing significance (2002, 270).

In producing the management plan, therefore, previous surveys
were consulted, including those of buildings, archaeological
sites and wildlife, along with oral history which for a place of
such recent historical importance is a major consideration.

The second point to consider concerns the need to manage
Robben Island to take account of the subtle traces of its recent
and traumatic history. As Clark states, this is a vulnerable
landscape:

> Small losses in a landscape, the lack of maintenance of
> buildings, incidental damage by tourists, all of which may

be minor in their own right, yet when taken cumulatively over say fifty years, can result in significant loss. Most of the damage is not deliberate; it is usually done because we have other priorities in mind and are not aware of the consequences. Often it is also the result of competing values (ibid., 274).

The limestone quarry is an example of this. This is the place where prisoners worked without sunglasses to protect them from the glare that came off the white rock face. Now tourist buses take visitors into the quarry where this story is told. Yet the rock faces are no longer white, having been darkened by bus fumes. One set of values therefore – the need for visitor access – is competing with another – the experience of the visitor as reflected in the landscape (ibid.). It is in aspects of site management such as this that the management plan is of most benefit.

Continued use, or adaptive re-use

Let us begin here with a case study. Take Upper Heyford, a former RAF and USAF airbase in Oxfordshire, discussed briefly in Chapter 3. This was clearly of national importance, as explained in English Heritage's national review of Cold War monuments (Cocroft 2001). Yet English Heritage chose to recommend the scheduling of only a very small component of the site, leaving the rest unprotected and – in theory at least – available for redevelopment. The Victor Alert area of Hardened Aircraft Shelters (Figure 4.2) was considered appropriate for in situ preservation because:

Hardened Aircraft Shelters (HAS) were the most distinctive military airfield structure constructed during the late 1970s and 1980s, their architecture reflecting contemporary NATO policy to harden and dull-down their key airfields.

The whole complex within the 'Victoria Alert' is considered to be of national importance to retain the functional relationship between structures and their period setting. This group of nine shelters also reflects what would have been the first level response by NATO to a pre-emptive nuclear strike by the Warsaw Pact. The group also represents the first phase of HAS construction in the UK and was associated with the F-111E, whose all weather capability made it one of NATO's key assets during the 1970s. Other buildings within the group are an integral part of the complex and illustrate other hardened building types. Its double fence and steel Brunswick tower are characteristic of the security surrounding a nuclear weapons area, and these should be included in the scheduling (Cocroft 2001).

The remainder of the site did not in the view of English Heritage lend itself to the management regime that scheduling would inevitably impose on this extensive area. It was felt that scheduling would be appropriate here only if the intention was to preserve the site unchanged, out of everyday use. For a site of this size that was considered likely to be unsustainable and impossible to achieve. Instead it was felt that the best course would be to manage the site in its entirety in partnership with the local authority, the site's owners and potential developers. That way a viable and sustainable future could be secured, but with recognition given to the impact this site has had, both socially and at landscape scale. Some roads could be retained; the footprint of the airfield could be maintained, with the line of the runway adopted by some arterial route through the site, retaining the key sight-lines along and through Upper Heyford; and yet setting apart a few key structures which could be

Fig. 4.2. The Victor Alert area at USAF Upper Heyford (Oxfordshire), built during the 1970s to accommodate armed F111 ground attack aircraft.

designated and protected as historic buildings or monuments, though not to the detriment of the site's economic viability.

A similar case has been made for other Cold War airbases, such as at Greenham Common, where the technical site now survives as a business park, the flying field has been returned to common land, the Ground-launched cruise missiles Alert and Maintenance Area is a scheduled monument (as discussed above), and there are plans to use the former control tower as an interpretative centre for the landscape as a whole. The business park makes numerous and significant references to the technical site that preceded it: much of the footprint remains, road names have been retained as have some of the buildings.

A third example is Calshot (Hampshire), at the mouth of the Solent. This former World War I sea plane base has been adapted to serve as an outdoor leisure facility, owned and managed by Hampshire County Council. Within the Grade II* listed hangars are a velodrome, dry ski slope and climbing wall. Other places have been developed as museum facilities: the Science Museum now occupies the former airbase at Wroughton, near Swindon (Wiltshire), while Priddy's Hard near Gosport (Hampshire) is now home to Explosion!, a Royal Naval armaments museum.

Most former military sites – as with industrial sites – are what are generally called 'brownfield', a term some in the planning sector equate with potential for re-use and redevelopment. And as these examples show, that can indeed be the case. However, the point here is that cultural heritage values will also have relevance, and will need to be accommodated in determining future use. This comes back to informed conservation – understanding what is there, and what values a place has, before reaching a conclusion. Cultural heritage is only one consideration of course, but it is one that needs to be set alongside all others.

Symbolic representation

In some cases, where the site itself has been removed, some symbolic representation may remain, or may be introduced, for example, by contemporary artists (Figure 4.3). At one extreme these reminders exist as war memorials to those that served locally, and perhaps lost their lives in the local area. At the other extreme is the folk memory sometimes retained in the

Fig. 4.3. A contemporary representation of combat on the Western Front.

most subtle of ways, such as photographs in a local pub, or a street or house name. But in the middle are a whole host of artistic interventions that often quite effectively and adequately represent former use of the area.

The most basic of representations exist at Greenham Common, where the former runways have been removed, both to return the former flying field to common land, but also to generate aggregate for new roads in the Newbury area. But rather than remove all of the runways, a small section was left at the point where the main runway is crossed by a taxiway, leaving a small (150-200 m) central 'cross'. It is rather a poor representation as the cross has been truncated almost to the point where it forms a rounded hexagon, but the intention was there.

145

In Berlin an area of the Wall – and specifically the strip between the two walls, the no-man's-land where only rabbits survived, being too light to release the trip wires or detonate mines – was used as the location for 'Rabbit Sign' by Karla Sachse. In 1996 thirty-two artists were invited by the Berlin Senate to take part in a competition encouraging artistic interpretations of former border crossing points. Some were commissioned, including 'Rabbit Sign'. Here, to recall their peaceful subversion of the border strip, 120 life-size silhouettes of rabbits were cut from sheet brass and stuck onto the surface of streets and pavements on the site of a former crossing (Feversham and Schmidt 1999, 156). As the authors explain:

> It is interesting to recall that an East Berlin children's club run by an artist friend of Sachse's used to hold a 'rabbit party', and raise the 'rabbit flag' – an oblique reference to the idiomatic German expression '*das Hasenpanier ergreifen*' (i.e. showing the rabbit flag = running away), an expression so archaic that the Stasi failed to grasp its subversive undertones (ibid.).

Also in Berlin, the site of Checkpoint Charlie – the front-line of the Cold War, at times at least – is now marked by two tall steel pillars, each displaying luminous photographic images, one of an American soldier facing east, and one of a Soviet soldier facing west.

But as Feversham and Schmidt point out in retrospect, this competition – these interventions – can also be interpreted as

> ... a rash of anodyne artworks that look set fair to be submerged by the life of the city. ... they seem to be lightweight gestures, neither bold nor beautiful. Nor indeed do any of the official artistic projects engage with the

existing architectonic substance – they are, in fact, purely mnemonic artefacts ...

In contrast, it is the unofficial artistic actions which, by virtue of their spontaneity and directness, are often more arresting than the well-meaning projects processed by committees, experts and politicians (1999, 156-60).

As Feversham and Schmidt conclude, artistic interventions are important in the context of conservation in two vital respects:

1. the awareness of monuments [a loose translation of the German *Denkmalbewusstein*]; and
2. mediation and re-conceptualisation.

Art possesses the power to promote a dialogue between past and future memories of a structure, helping to ensure its contemporary relevance and preventing it becoming moribund, static. ... There is an argument that contemporary art has a vital, if largely unsung part to play in this respect, acting as an *agent provocateur* in re-energizing spaces which by virtue of their very historicity are in danger of being perceived as sacrosanct (1999, 166).

As a final example here I want to return to South Africa and briefly mention a project at District Six in Cape Town, the aim of which was to create artistic interventions on land from which coloured inhabitants had been cleared under the terms of the apartheid regime's 1966 Group Areas Act. This land was marked for redevelopment following the clearance, though the site has since remained empty and undeveloped (see Malan and Soudien 2002 for details). The 1997 District Six Public Sculpture Project (Soudien and Mayer nd) aimed to create something which would allow former residents to symbolically re-occupy the area, and stand until redevelopment began. Some years later, and the archaeology of some of these artistic interventions remains.

Bedford and Murinik (nd) describe the background to this Heritage Day event:

> The project created the opportunity for a broad range of people, connected and/or implicated on various levels within the histories of District Six, whether directly or indirectly, to find and convey meaning within this place. It gives artists the opportunity to declare worth to a land and its people who were victims of the official system that made them vanish. This is a rare accomplishment. The works produced for Heritage Day in 1997 evoked remembrance, respect, dignity and worth to those things absent. The public projects also evoked a sense of the tragic consequences of apartheid's barbaric system, of a deep sadness and moments of discomfort. They provided spaces within which to grieve and to find strength and solace in that scarred land. They were beacons that declared a history in the process of being boldly reclaimed (ibid., 13).

Recording

Often where it is decided that sites will be demolished in advance of redevelopment, or as in the case of Greenham Common, that the flying field will revert to common land and some of the buildings be removed, recording will be recommended, generally paid for by the developer (the 'polluter pays' principle again). Sometimes – in England at least – English Heritage survey teams will undertake this work, but often consultants with a specialism in this area are commissioned. Recording can take one or more of the following approaches, depending on the nature of the site:

148

1. Aerial photographic survey, looking to provide a rapid and overarching view of architectural styles, plan form and condition. For some sites this can then be compared to earlier aerial photographs to produce a 'then and now' record. Increasingly, video is being used for recording sites.

2. A 'characterisation' based on a diversity of sources, including aerial photographs and historical maps, supplemented with a rapid walkover survey, providing an overview of the site, its plan form components, architecture and evolution. This level of survey would generally be used as the basis for discussing development proposals at a strategic level. A recent study adopted this approach for RAF Scampton (Lincolnshire).

3. Photographic recording, at medium or large format to generate an archive, generally then placed within English Heritage's National Monuments Record at Swindon (NMRC). Photographic recording was undertaken at a World War II prisoner of war camp in Lincolnshire prior to its demolition. Wall art will often be recorded during photographic survey.

4. A buildings survey, documenting the building and where appropriate comparing that record with archive material. One of the redundant hangars at former USAF Greenham Common was recorded prior to its demolition. This approach will generally also include photographic survey.

5. Archaeological study: this can involve surveying of field remains, and – in theory – excavation, though this has been used sparingly on recent military sites to date.

Recording is undertaken – often within the terms of planning guidance or to meet the requirements of some statutory constraint – to create a record prior to the object of that record being lost or removed. Some military and industrial sites, for example, are so specialised, and their structures so unsuited to any form of use other than that for which they were originally designed, that redevelopment will be the only sustainable option. Of course if a building or site was of critical significance – a critical asset – and if resources and a management plan were in place, then retention might be an option. Generally, though, that is not the case.

At Thurleigh (Bedfordshire) the Royal Aircraft Establishment consisted of a series of buildings on a compact but remote site. These were specialised structures including wind tunnels for testing aircraft engines. The entire site was considered of national importance. One of the wind tunnels has been retained by a Formula 1 team, while others have been bought by American aviation companies for use in aircraft testing in the United States. The rest of the site will be demolished. Here English Heritage undertook a detailed photographic survey prior to sale, while a consultant produced a history of the site and a characterisation study based on field observation and archives (Francis 2003). Oral history will be another source in some cases, though not at Thurleigh. A similar site at Farnborough (Hampshire) is to be developed in part as a heritage centre, with its wind tunnels serving as the focus for visitors. The site recently hosted a day of aviation-related artistic performances – the Artists Airshow event, 2004. Again recording has been commissioned prior to work starting on the regeneration.

What to record is another issue, and while briefs are routinely prepared for recording sites prior to their removal, and including all built and buried structures, there is an argument that these studies should be research driven to a greater degree. Research agenda now exist for a diversity of subject and geographical areas, and these documents provide the context in which resource and research issues can be best addressed. In *Modern Military Matters* (Schofield 2004), for example, questions are raised and priorities established. One priority is to determine what archaeological excavation can contribute to our understanding of recent military sites. We know what field survey can contribute (e.g. McOmish et al. 2001), but what about buried remains? Through work in France on World War I sites (e.g. Saunders 2002a) and excavations of crashed aircraft, the potential seems fairly obvious, however.

Summary

This chapter has briefly explored the world of heritage protection, as it has been applied specifically to recent military sites. The chapter is a case study, illustrating the various options and their implications for sites of all types and all periods. What sets recent military material culture apart, and what I hope this chapter has managed to convey, is the challenge that these sites present, both in terms of the scale of military installations (airfields for example, where the runway alone is typically three kilometres in length), the numbers of sites, the specialised buildings, designed and built for very specific purposes and which almost by definition prevent any other use without destroying the character of the original, and the health and safety connotations, either from pollution (Kuletz 1998), or ammunition.

While the focus here has been on England, it is worth stressing that while laws may be different, many of these principles apply equally across Europe and further afield. Through the Council of Europe, funding initiatives such as Culture 2000, and the European Archaeological Colloquium, organisations are working together to ensure that the cultural heritage is afforded appropriate and adequate treatment and protection. Above all else is the principle that in order to manage something effectively, one must first understand it. That is largely what the first four chapters of this book have been about, to the point of deciding if and how to afford the site protection. What happens after that will be the subject of Chapter 5, looking at interpretation and presentation.

5

Presentation/interpretation

Many places that saw conflict, or that played a supporting role, for example as training grounds, remain in military use, or have been bought privately and now have a new lease of life. Comparatively few of these sites are accessible to the public, and those that are have either been left as they were found, surviving as ruins or buried remains, or have been subject to some heritage interpretation scheme or initiative: a museum may exist on the site, an audio-tour may be available, as might interpretative panels or a guidebook. In some places the interpretation is purely descriptive, telling visitors what they see and giving historical context; in other places the interpretation is more focussed, or designed to challenge and provoke. In this chapter I outline some of the principles that underlie the interpretation of sites of conflict, and finish with a few select examples. These examples are indicative of some of the schemes that exist around the world. The selection is based entirely on personal experience.

Hot interpretation

Much has been written about how we interpret what we see, and how those responsible for presenting cultural heritage create displays and exhibits, or manage monuments, to take account of the diversity of demands and responses that society will inevitably create (e.g. Uzzell 1989; Uzzell 1998; Uzzell and Ballantyne 1999). Should we present the archaeology of warfare at all is one question. And if we should, then how can it be presented in a balanced and objective way?

A comparison can be found with the argument about motoring heritage and museums: 'Do cars belong in museums?', Graves Brown has asked (1996). Here a centenary was the opportunity (or the excuse) to promote what the author described as the 'picturesque fiction of one hundred years of Britain's motor industry [that] largely ignores fact and controversy'. Interpretation was 'cool', dispassionate and uncontroversial, and far from the hot interpretation that some may prefer. It avoided arguments about environmental pollution, both relating to car use and the ever-extending road schemes that it required. This point about hot interpretation will be especially relevant to interpretations of conflict, or anything that involves human suffering and hardship, but in fact extends to issues that have immediate relevance and stir emotions. The term originates with Abelson (1963) who called thinking about vital issues which have an emotional or affective dimension, 'hot cognitions'. Uzzell explains:

> This is not to argue that decision-making can be divided into two types: cool and dispassionate, and hot and emotional. Rather, it is to suggest that because we are human and not automatons, issues which involve personal values, beliefs and interests will nevertheless excite a degree of emotional arousal, even though contemplated in a calm and level-headed way (1989, 34).

Tilden has commented on this, noting how interpretation is:

> an educational activity which aims to reveal meanings and relationships through the use of original objects, by firsthand experience, and by illustrative media, rather than simply to communicate factual information (1957, 8).

Tilden also argues that 'the chief aim of interpretation is not instruction but provocation', and that interpretation must 'address itself to the whole man rather than any phase' (ibid., 9), referring to the need to include people's feelings and emotions.

Elsewhere (in press) I have argued for engaging and affective displays that convey the sense and meaning of conflict, and some of the examples that follow illustrate what I mean by this, and how such presentations and interpretations can be achieved. Uzzell (1989) presents others, such as Oradour-sur-Glane, in central France, where on 10 June 1944 an SS Unit belonging to Das Reich Division shot the men of the town while women and children were kept in the church. An explosive device was subsequently detonated in the church, and the women and children shot as they escaped. The town – houses, barns, cars – was then destroyed. In all, 642 people died at Oradour-sur-Glane. How the town is interpreted has been discussed by Uzzell (1989, 37-40) with a critique offered by Olivier (2001). Interpretation has changed over the years, and significantly since Uzzell's (1989) essay, a new visitor centre has been built (see Stone 2004 for a contemporary view).

In 1989 Jacques Hivernaud was a guide who presented the events of the day with intensity and feeling, having lost several relatives in the massacre. The town itself was as it was left – cars still abandoned and buildings burnt out. Small artefacts – spectacles and watches – complete the picture. But as Uzzell states:

> We must not forget that for the new town, built less than a kilometre away, the mere presence of the destroyed and abandoned town is interpretation. The environment itself is a book which can be read by those who choose to read, irrespective of the activities of a group of people called interpreters (ibid., 38).

5. Presentation/interpretation

Yet all is not as it seems at Oradour-sur-Glane. Olivier (2001, 185), for example, considers what happens when the vestiges themselves invent history. Dr Desorteaux arrived in Oradour on 10 June only to be stopped by the SS and forced to park his car in the town square. He was then led with other men to the barns and killed. The significance of the car could therefore tie in directly to this very personal story of the massacre. However, contrary to how history is presented, the car in the town square isn't his at all. After the massacre, the doctor's brother came to fetch the car and take it home, where it remained. The car that became Dr Desorteaux's was in fact the wine seller's car. It was blocking an access when the fire service arrived, so was removed to the square. As I will explain later, authenticity is a key consideration in interpreting sites of conflict.

Hot interpretation can be seen at World War I sites along the Western Front. Here the material legacies of the war – trench systems, tunnels, shell holes – can be viewed, and first-hand experiences read in affective and informative interpretation centres where photographs and words convey the real horror of the Front. Given that the majority of visitors have some family connection or at least know of someone who either died or suffered emotionally as a result of the war, this is all the more immediate. This is not true of all conflict, however. Uzzell (1999, 18) has described the difficulty with interpreting Cold War sites in this way, as they represent a placeless war; a war that was everywhere and nowhere – a war where sites are not in themselves scenes of conflict and death. An example of how this can be achieved – at Greenham Common – is described below.

Punctum

Barthes (2000) says much about the punctum, the thing that 'holds' him in a photograph. He notes for example how the punctum should be revealed only after the fact, when 'the photograph is no longer in front of me and I think back on it' (2000, 53). The punctum is very often a detail. It can also be a shock or a surprise; something even the photographer hadn't seen or intended. Finally 'it is an addition: it is what I add to the photograph and *what is nonetheless already there*' (ibid., 55; italics in original). This then is how we read photographs: some pictures prick us and strike a chord; they are memorable and remain with us. The same is true of museums and interpretative displays. Something we see will act as a punctum, and for a child visiting a site of conflict, or a museum, that punctum may have a lasting affect. So what makes a punctum?

In a sense this will be beyond definition, as it will be in part culturally constituted and in part based on personal experience, personality and preference. We cannot just put things in a display that we expect people to remember and to be shocked or surprised by – some will and some won't. Some things do have greater potential than others, however, and here I mention just two examples. One is the child's lunch box recovered from the rubble at Hiroshima after the atomic bomb fell in 1945. Wherever this lunch box is displayed it provokes a reaction, and of course children relate to its poignancy immediately. A second example is the many objects removed from prisoners at concentration camps during World War II. Weinberg and Elieli (1995) show the hair shorn from the heads of female inmates and displayed now at the museum at Auschwitz, and the shoes confiscated from prisoners at Majdanek. In the Holocaust Museum in Washington DC these shoes are displayed under the words:

> We are the shoes, we are the last witnesses.
> We are the shoes from grandchildren and grandfathers,
> From Prague, Paris and Amsterdam,
> And because we are only made of fabric and leather,

5. Presentation/interpretation

And not of blood and flesh, each one of us avoided the
hellfire.

Moses Schulstein (1911-1981)
Yiddish poet

In interpreting the material culture of conflict, how we present the sites matters, as does the approach to artefacts and
possessions. But authenticity is key. Dr Desorteaux's car may
be a punctum to some, but for the wrong reasons. Things need
to prick visitors, but they need to be authentic as well.

Voices, words and people

First-hand experiences are central in conveying sense of place,
and interpreting past events. Museums and interpretative centres often now use this medium to convey experience or to
present a particular narrative. In some museums – in Flanders
Fields at Ypres, for example – visitors take on the identity of a
real person that experienced the conflict, and follow that person's story through the museum, to its conclusion at the end.
Generally, though, experience is presented through photographs, war art (as at the Imperial War Museum in London),
sound archives and recordings accessible at listening posts, and
written accounts, both in the museums and available as books.
But interpreting past events is perhaps most easily achieved
through these first-hand accounts, and one example illustrates
this point.

In 1996 the historian Martin Gilbert was asked by his students (studying for their MA in Holocaust Studies at University
College, London) to take them to the places they had learnt
about on the course. In his book *Holocaust Journey: travelling
in search of the past* (1998) Gilbert presents the diary of that
visit. He describes visits to many of the places – camps, ghet-
toes, Jewish quarters and places where individual and isolated

tragedies occurred – and the powerful effect of the first-hand accounts that he read to his students. The combined effect of their sense of place – partly enhanced by their educational and cultural background – and the accounts of those that suffered there, or those that survived, was too much for some to take; and some students did not complete the trip. It was Gilbert's readings, at the very sites of the atrocities, that gave these places such poignancy, and made the experience so affective.

The general point here is that sites (in the sense of monuments and places) documenting troubled pasts, and especially those which involved human suffering, should attempt to convey a sense of the place to visitors. To talk of ghosts may seem unscientific, but it has relevance (Bell 1997), as Gilbert illustrates citing John Izbicki's account of the reinauguration of the restored Orianenburger Strasse Synagogue in Berlin on 7 May 1995, where he had prayed as a young boy before emigrating to Britain in 1939:

> We all sat outside, on the ground where two-thirds of the original building once stood. This empty space, where the main hall of the synagogue used to be, is to be left as a lasting scar of history. It is the remaining one-third that has been transformed into a museum, a place for researchers to come and study the history of German Jewry. The roof of that one-third is adorned now, as it was before, with two golden cupolas that shine like beacons across the Berlin skyline. As I listened to the speeches of eminent personalities and looked up at the windows of the restored building, I thought I saw – and certainly felt – the presence of so many others who had once prayed there (quoted in Gilbert 1998, 36).

5. Presentation/interpretation

Three examples

Blitz experiences

Wartime monuments enable World War II and Cold War sites to be experienced by a public who are increasingly knowledgeable about and interested in the material culture of these recent historical events. But as with places like Oradour-sur-Glane, engaging museum displays have a complementary and significant role. The experience of the Blitz, brought to life to varying degrees by the Blitz Experience at the Imperial War Museum, and another at the London at War Museum (critically reviewed by Noakes 1997), for example, provides a focus for exploring landscapes of the Blitz in contemporary London (Holmes 1997). To take the last first, the London at War display encourages the visitor to understand the Blitz by 'experiencing it'; to share the wartime experience, to 'see it, feel it, breathe it ... be part of those momentous days'. As Noakes describes it (ibid., 96-7),

> Descending in a rickety lift, the visitor emerges into a reconstruction of a tube shelter, where she or he can sit on original bales of wartime blankets, to watch a collage of wartime newsreels .... Emerging from the Tube shelter, the visitor next walks along a corridor lined with photos of London during the Blitz and newspaper headlines of the time. At the end of this corridor the visitor can choose to enter an Anderson shelter, where she or he can listen to recorded sounds of an air raid, look at an exhibition, or pass on to the centrepiece of the museum, the 'Blitz Experience'.

The Imperial War Museum's 'Blitz Experience' is rather different:

> Visitors are ushered into it by a guide, entering through a

159

small dark doorway to find themselves in a reconstruction of a London brick-built shelter. The shelterers are urged on into the shelter by the taped voice of George, a local air-raid warden. As the shelter fills more voices appear on the tape, all with strong London accents. Some talk about their day while others complain of lack of sleep. As the bombs begin to fall, George leads them in a hearty rendition of 'Roll Out the Barrel'. As the bombs get closer, George's daughter Val becomes hysterical, her screams gradually drowning out the singing. A bomb drops uncomfortably close and the shelter reverberates. Everything goes quiet.

The shelterers are then helped outside by the museum guide, whose flashlight plays around the devastated street that they are now standing in. In front of them lies an upturned pram, its front wheel still spinning .... As the shelterers leave blitzed London to become museum visitors once more, their last experience of the Blitz is George's fading voice saying 'Don't forget us' (ibid., 95-6).

There are common factors here. Both experiences involve damage to property not people. Emerging from the experience at London at War, what may at first be thought to be bodies are, on closer inspection, mannequins from a bombed shop, though the initial impression may be deliberate. Also, both experiences are of large communal shelters, even though these accommodated only a small percentage of London's population. As Noakes puts it (ibid.), the experiences represent a sanitised version of a minority experience presented as a majority experience, and the London at War display bears little resemblance to the Tube shelter recalled by a former shelterer in Calder's *The People's War* (1969, 183), who described a place where 'the stench was frightful, urine and excrement mixed with strong carbolic, sweat and dirty, unwashed humanity'. Yet despite obvious limitations in telling the typical Blitz experience pre-cisely as it was, these are engaging displays. There are personal accounts to be read, photographs to be seen, and – not too far away from either Museum – bombsites to be visited, such as the ruined churches of St Mary Aldermanbury, St Dunstan-in-the-East and Christ Church.

District Six

What happened to District Six under the apartheid regime is well documented (Hall 2001, Malan and Soudien 2002). Having been declared a whites-only area under Proclamation 43 of the Group Areas Act (1966), virtually the entire district was physi-cally erased from the map. Some 62,000 people had previously occupied the area, according to government figures, which also indicated that three-quarters of these were tenants, and all but a thousand were classified as 'coloured' (i.e. of mixed race) in the terms of the Population Registration Act. By 1978 some coloured families were still resident in the District, which by this time had become a rallying point for opposition to the forced removals that were taking place throughout South Af-rica. By 1984 the removals were complete. All that remained was the scar separating Cape Town from its suburbs: South Africa's Hiroshima, as one commentator described it; alterna-tively, 'the preserve of South Africa and all of humanity' (Nagra pers. comm.).

In 1986 BP (Southern Africa) announced its intention to rebuild District Six as South Africa's first open residential area, once again attempting to impose policies on communities with-out consultation. BP's proposal further focused an already strong opposition and stimulated the formation of the Hands Off District Six campaign (HODS), an alliance of organisations and former residents which campaigned for the abolition of the Group Areas Act prior to any redevelopment. Abolition of the

Act has since happened and in August 1997 a land court ruling gave the area back to former residents.

District Six today is an eloquent symbol of the policy of racial segregation that dominates South Africa's recent history, and of the sense of community which the apartheid regime attempted to destroy. District Six was once heterogeneous and cohesive; there was no residential segregation between classes; and there existed a level of tolerance among people that could accommodate a range of religious and political beliefs (le Grange 1996, 8). This state of affairs was unacceptable to the apartheid regime. District Six is now empty – forty-four hectares of scrub which effectively hides the drama of the natural red earth, which 'bled' at the time of the removals, but which does at least protect a rich and significant archaeological record documenting the history of the District's occupation and ultimately its clearance. Furthermore, there remains a strong District Six community on the Cape Flats, and the plan now is to rebuild theDistrict, returning some former residents alongside first-time occupants.

> In 1989 ex-residents of District Six envisaged a museum to commemorate the area and honour the people who fought against the forced removals and Group Areas Act. On 10 December 1994, the District Six Museum opened with its first exhibition 'Streets – Retracing the Past'. The museum provides a space for the community to come together and share their experiences and retrace their memories. The District Six Museum is a reminder that forced removals must never happen again (Museum brochure, undated).

The District Six Museum is more than just a display. For a start it acts as the focus of a now dispersed community, and for this reason its location in the old Methodist church on the edge of the District is particularly apposite. It was this church, also called 'the freedom church', that took a stand against the injustices of the Group Areas Act and other apartheid legislation. It now serves as a meeting place, an educational resource, and a point of contact. The museum also has an important political role in the District's redevelopment, as well as acting as a conduit for narratives and personal accounts (publishing some of its own works and selling others), oral history, sound archives, and artefacts, such as those from archaeological excavations undertaken by the University of Cape Town in recent years. It was also closely involved in the public sculpture project in 1997, designed in part to reclaim the District for former residents.

The museum is interactive. Former residents are encouraged to sign a cloth, which is later embroidered. Much of the ground floor is taken up with a map of District Six prior to the clearances, with the road names marked. Here former residents sign their names and number the houses where they once lived. The museum also houses a huge photographic archive. When this was first shown publicly, it led to a celebration of life among former residents; singing, arguing and debating. And among the museum staff are former residents who will discuss the District with visitors, adding colour to an already engaging interpretive experience. What the museum does not overtly do, however, is to show the horror of the removals. As many visitors have remarked, the power of the museum lies in the fact that it has a celebratory air about it. There are no 'in your face bulldozers'; rather people are remembering themselves as a community, in a museum which is essentially a homely place.

The District Six Museum currently receives comparatively few visitors; only around fifty overseas tourists a day visit, for example, mostly arranged through tour operators. Fewer still visit the District itself, probably because of concerns about personal security, even though the interpretation which the

museum provides prepares visitors well for touring it. To facili-
tate this, a leaflet has been produced by the museum which
provides a self-guided tour taking in the existing churches and
mosques; the one terrace of cottages that survived the clearance
and which today gives an impression of District Six's original
appearance; the cobbled streets, in many ways the centre of
district life; and the foundations of front steps from which
people all over the District watched the passing scene.

Proposals to redevelop District Six have been under discussion for some years. It is a controversial matter and one which
the local community will have to resolve with politicians and
city planners if a mutually acceptable solution is to be found.
From a conservation perspective, it is important that the character of the District, and at least some of its physical remains,
are retained to work alongside the museum in interpreting the
past, for three main reasons:

First, for the sense of belonging such areas provide for their
former inhabitants. The District Six Museum, for example, has
served to galvanise a community that was scattered among the
townships in the years following the passing of the Group Areas
Act, while the forty-four hectares of empty ground (excepting
the churches and mosques that remain) has, throughout the
apartheid years and beyond, acted as a daily reminder of the
removals, to Capetonians and visitors alike.

Second, the 'lessons from history' argument, that the social
injustice of the forced removals must be kept in the past. There
is also the hope that lessons from South Africa will eventually
attain wider geographical and geopolitical significance and influence.

Third, for the reason that increasingly people want to know
about the recent past, and in particular about the momentous
events of the later twentieth century. What happened in South
Africa under the apartheid regime constitutes a major episode

in recent world history, and District Six tells that story arguably better than anywhere else.

What is finally agreed will need to be sustainable in the long term, and for this reason alone the strategic location of the vacant land, the size of the area and the increasing need for affordable inner-city housing suggest that a significant amount of development will be necessary, and this is perhaps appropriate in the circumstances.

Rehousing those forcibly removed sounds attractive, but not all individuals removed can (or perhaps even want to) return, and new developments such as the Technikon – built originally for white students only – cannot simply be removed. But as le Grange (1996, 15) has sensibly argued, District Six can still be used as a model for how to address the wrong-doings of the past and as a way by which to heal a divided city. Of course this would require the participation of the affected community and the concerted political will of government to deal sensitively with the planning and implementation of a reconstruction programme. Three specific aspects of this 'model' can be identified:

First, it is important that the future development of the District draws upon the urban planning traditions of its past. For example: the fine-grained street network; the mixed land-use development; a mix of housing types to ensure social heterogeneity; the street as community space; and the population density that shaped the area and which can be reinterpreted and adapted to serve contemporary requirements (after le Grange 1996). The surviving churches and mosques could serve as foci within a redesigned District Six, with one of them housing the museum.

Second, views and vistas will be important, particularly for former residents revisiting the District. To this end le Grange (1996) produced designs to retain as open space an area either side of the sloping and cobbled Horsley Street which uses mounds of rubble to obscure the foreground, yet showing glimpses of the city, a view that residents would have had. This area also includes the site of one of the three excavations undertaken in the district by the University of Cape Town; artefacts from these excavations could remain on view at the museum.

Third, places of memory should be (and in fact are being) considered, to serve for example as areas for quiet reflection and play. In 1993, the District Six Museum Foundation called a public meeting to get support from the community to set aside land in District Six for such 'memorial parks'. This remains on the agenda at the time of writing and would be important for many reasons, such as allowing easy access to the District for those who cannot or choose not to return as residents. As we have seen, the front steps of houses, from which residents watched the passing scene, survive in some areas, along with original cobbling. In terms of presenting and remembering past events, these steps and cobbling are arguably the most meaningful of all material remains surviving within the District and would be an important component of such 'memorial parks'.

In summary, District Six is an evocative and an important place, both for former residents and for visitors. For those who understand its significance its atmosphere is tangible, obviously so for former residents but for visitors too. What happens to the District matters to all these people, but most significantly of course it matters to the future generations who will visit and interpret it. For those future visitors the steps, the cobbles and the bare red earth may be the most powerfully symbolic of all its material remains, and for that reason alone the arguments for their retention are compelling.

Greenham Common

The example of Greenham Common is not so much a matter of what has been achieved, as what could be done. We have already seen what survives at Greenham Common, and how significant the site is both for its World War II, and in particular for its Cold War heritage. To recap, the former technical site is now a business park, which follows the plan-form of the earlier site and has re-used some of its buildings; roads remain the same, on the same alignment and with the same names. The flying field was originally common land, and since the USAF withdrew this has now reverted to common, with open public access throughout. The runways, hardstandings and taxiways have been removed, the aggregate used for the new Newbury by-pass which, like Greenham before it, was the subject of considerable environmental protest and opposition. Finally, there is the control tower on the north side of the airfield and the Ground-launched cruise missiles Alert and Maintenance Area (GAMA) on the airfield's south-west side. Consensus seems to support the idea of public interpretation at Greenham, but how, and where?

What exist to date are a number of disparate presentations. In Newbury Museum are some artefacts related to the military occupation of the site and opposition towards it. Within the business park is New Greenham Arts, including their gallery space which often includes Greenham-inspired and -derived work (some of this has in the past been exhibited in the control tower or other buildings close by [e.g. Kippin 2001]). The Web contains a wealth of information, and notable of the sites with oral historical material is the Imperial War Museum's website (www.iwm.org.uk). Finally there is the Peace Garden close to the base's main entrance at what the Peace Women called Yellow Gate. Here land was purchased and a garden designed and built to commemorate the actions of women in opposing nuclear arms.

What could be done goes far beyond that, and over the past two years archaeology undergraduates at Southampton University taking the Heritage Management option have used

Greenham Common as the basis for producing a 'mock' management plan for the site as part of their assessed work. This has generated a wealth of imaginative and exciting schemes which seek to balance out the regenerative potential of the site, and especially GAMA, within the wider context of Greenham Common's Cold War landscape, with the need for some objective and informative interpretation. Does GAMA require interpretation boards or displays, for example? How can the control tower sit alongside this scheme, and could it in fact provide the interpretative space, enabling GAMA to remain unchanged, in its raw and robust form? What about the fences that surround GAMA? These are the only fences remaining of those that at one time dominated the visual and perceptual landscape on the Common. Should the fences be kept, continuing to separate the missile shelters from their landscape context and from the people who now seek to understand and explore them; or should they be removed, thus effectively re-uniting this area of the site with the rest of the Common? I have discussed one possibility for this (Schofield and Anderton 2000), while students have come up with many more imaginative and challenging ideas than mine.

I will not offer any solution here; merely an invitation, in view of all I have said, to consider Greenham Common, perhaps to visit, and to think through the various possibilities. It is a challenging site, but certainly not unique. As with all these places, balance is the key: providing something that retains the character, the aura of the place, but is informative and interesting, and perhaps in some cases where sustainable solutions are needed, allows the scheme to survive. Mixed use may be the answer, as at Chatham Dockyard in Kent, where the visitor attraction sits (literally) alongside craft and light industry, ensuring that the site as a whole remains buoyant.

5. Presentation/interpretation

Summary

To summarise, (re)presentations of the past should be:

Accurate. Displays should aim to tell the story as it was, and not some sanitised or diluted version or fabrication of the truth. Stories can of course be tailored for younger visitors, and some sensitive information can be effectively hidden in the more technical guidebooks or 'top-shelf' display facilities, if that is considered appropriate. On occasion, controversy – either about what happened or the implications of certain events or actions – will prevent a consensus of opinion, and in such cases displays may never materialise. This proved to be the case with the now well documented disagreements over the Smithsonian's Hiroshima display (see, e.g., Gieryn 1998; Perkins 1999; and Linenthal 1995).

Facilitating. As we have seen already,

> sense of place is not a given, and therefore cannot necessarily be passed on only by interpretation. It is created by individuals, and the aim of displays should be to give people the means to develop their own appreciation of significance. Interpretation ... should facilitate .... [There is also a need for] sense of place to be 'owned' and to grow out of individual experience, needs and perceptions .... The sense of discovery is vital. Residents and visitors – and scholars and interpreters – should jointly participate and share their perceptions (Fairclough forthcoming).

Engaging. Presenting troubled pasts will be most effectively achieved by emphasising human experience. This can be achieved in different ways: the value of written accounts; the use as guides of former prisoners at Robben Island and former

169

residents at Oradour-sur-Glane and District Six; audio-visual techniques, and the simple and uncomplicated use of photographs; and the use of fictional characters, represented by for example by Val and her growing hysteria in the underground shelter in the Imperial War Museum's Blitz Experience. Another notable approach is for museum visitors to take on the identity of contemporary characters.

Respectful of past events. It is important that the correct balance is struck between providing a tourist 'attraction' and preserving the character of the place one is presenting to visitors. Plans to develop Auschwitz-Birkenau are an example: recently proposals have included enlarging the parking area, building a small by-pass around the main gate and a reception area opposite it, and converting the sauna (one of the few buildings to survive intact, excepting the huts) into a museum. Gilbert's reaction to these proposals was one of bewilderment, and in his view 'no doubt admirable from the museum curator's perspective, but incongruous after what [he and his students had] just seen' (1998, 173).

Signposts and symbols. It is important that engaging, accurate museum displays are not left alone in presenting troubled pasts, though they do of course have an important role to play. While these displays do provide the raw material through which visitors can gain insight into ordinary lives and personal experiences, the places themselves can be more powerful still in achieving these objectives, both in terms of the atmosphere or character of the place, and in its material remains. The open ground at District Six has extraordinary character, and has retained its sense of place and identity, a point reinforced on the 1997 Heritage Day holiday, when several thousand people 'reclaimed' District Six to look at art and listen to music. The ground also has the potential to be powerfully symbolic, the bare red earth acting as a reminder of the physical act of forced removal.

*

Dealing with the archaeology of recent conflict is never easy. Decisions concerning the development of wartime sites, or selection of some places for protection at the expense of others will be controversial. Some interpretative schemes won't satisfy the purists, while others may be interpreted by some as too highbrow, 'not enough fun', or too obscure. Falling short of anything definitive or inclusive, this chapter has sought to outline some of the principles by which places are presented and interpreted to the public, and has provided a few examples of what can be achieved.

The main point, though, is that these places lend themselves to interpretation, and that with levels of interest currently set high and rising there clearly is an audience for the attractions or experiences we seek to create. Not all sites can be treated in this way, nor should they be. Many former military sites are redundant, decaying and in private ownership. Oddly, given that these are the places generally without funding or conservation, they are often also the most evocative. It is the former control towers on abandoned airbases that veterans return to. It is in these out-of-the-way places that the 'ghosts of place' are most likely to be felt (Bell 1997).

Bibliography

Abelson, R.P. 1963. Computer simulation of 'hot' cognition. In Tomkins, S.S. and Messick, S. (eds), *Computer Simulation of Personality*, 277-98. Wiley: New York.

Accardo, G., Giani, E. and Giovagnoli, A. 2003. The risk map of Italian cultural heritage. *Journal of Architectural Conservation* 2, 41-57.

Addison, P. and Crang, J.A. (eds) 2000. *The Burning Blue: a new history of the Battle of Britain*. Pimlico: London.

Alexander, C. 1998. *Ironside's Line: the definitive guide to the General Headquarters Line planned for Great Britain in response to the threat of German invasion 1940-42*. Historic Military Press: Storrington.

Anderton, M. 2002. Social space and social control: analysing movement and management on modern military sites. In Schofield, J., Johnson, W.G. and Beck, C.M. (eds), *Matériel Culture: the archaeology of twentieth century conflict*, 189-98. Routledge: London and New York.

Anderton, M. and Schofield, J. 1999. Anti-aircraft gunsites – then and now. *Conservation Bulletin* 36, 11-13.

Aplin, G. 2002. *Heritage: identification, conservation, and management*. Oxford University Press.

Australian Heritage Commission, 2001. *Protecting Heritage Places Workbook*. Australian Heritage Commission and Commonwealth Department of the Environment and Heritage (Environment Australia). Available online at www.heritage.gov.au/protecting.html

Baker, F. 1993. The Berlin Wall: production, preservation and consumption of a twentieth century monument. *Antiquity* 67, 709-33.

Ballantyne, R. and Uzzell, D. 1993. Environmental mediation and hot interpretation: a case study of District Six, Cape Town. *Journal of Environmental Education* 24(3), 4-7.

Barthes, R. 2000 [1980]. *Camera Lucida: reflections on photography*. Vintage: London.

173

Beazley, O. in press. A paradox of peace: the Hiroshima Peace Memorial (Genbaku Dome) as world heritage. In Schofield, J. and Cocroft, W.D. (eds), *A Fearsome Heritage: the diverse legacies of the Cold War*. UCL.

Beck, C.M. 2002. The archaeology of scientific experiments at a nuclear testing ground. In Schofield, J., Johnson, W.G. and Beck, C.M. (eds), *Matériel Culture: the archaeology of twentieth century conflict*, 65-79. Routledge: London and New York.

Bedford, E. and Murinik, T. nd. Re-membering that place: public projects in District Six. In Soudien, C. and Mayer, R., *The District Six Public Sculpture Project*, 12-22. The District Six Museum Foundation: Cape Town.

Bell, M. 1997. The ghosts of place. *Theory and Society* 26, 813-36.

Black, J. 2004. Thanks for the memory: war memorials, spectatorship and the trajectories of commemoration 1919-2001. In Saunders, N. (ed.), *Matters of Conflict: material culture, memory and the First World War*, 134-48. Routledge: London.

Boulton, A. 2001. *Cood bay Forst Zinna* (film, privately distributed).

Bourke, J. 1999. *An Intimate History of Killing: face-to-face killing in twentieth century warfare*. Granta: London.

Bryson, B. 1996. *Notes from a Small Island*. Black Swan: London.

Buchli, V. and Lucas, G. 2001. *Archaeologies of the Contemporary Past*. Routledge: London and New York.

Byrne, D., Brayshaw, H. and Ireland, T. 2001. *Social Significance: a discussion paper*. NSW National Parks and Wildlife Service.

Calder, A. 1969. *The People's War 1939-45*. Cape: London.

Carman, J. (ed.) 1997. *Material Harm: archaeological studies of war and violence*. Cruithne Press: Glasgow.

Cave, N. 2000. Battlefield conservation: First International Workshop in Arras 29 February – 4 March 2000. *Battlefields Review* 10, 41-60.

Charlesworth, A.1994. Contesting places of memory: the case of Aushwitz. *Environment and Planning D: Society and Space* 12, 579-93.

Clark, K. 2001. *Informed Conservation: understanding historic buildings and their landscape for conservation*. English Heritage: London.

Clark, K. 2002. In small things remembered: significance and vulnerability in the management of Robben Island World Heritage Site. In Schofield, J., Johnson, W.G. and Beck, C.M. (eds), *Matériel Culture: the archaeology of twentieth century conflict*, 266-80. Routledge: London and New York.

Bibliography

Cocroft, W.D. 2000. *Dangerous Energy: the archaeology of gunpowder and military explosives manufacture.* English Heritage: London.

Cocroft, W.D. 2001. *Cold War Monuments: an assessment by the Monuments Protection Programme.* English Heritage: London (typescript report, available also on CD-Rom).

Cocroft, W.D. and Schofield, J. 2003. Images of the Cold War: combat art. *Conservation Bulletin* 44, 43-4.

Cocroft, W.D. and Thomas, R.J.C. 2003. *Cold War: building for nuclear confrontation 1946-89.* English Heritage: London.

Cocroft, W.D. in press. Defining the national archaeological character of Cold war remains. In Schofield, J. and Cocroft, W.D. (eds), *A Fearsome Heritage: the diverse legacies of the Cold War.* UCL.

Collings, M. 1999. *This is Modern Art.* Seven Dials: London.

Cotter, J. 2001. From reverse engineering to national treasure. *Fly-Past* January 2001, 51-4.

Crossland, Z. 2002. Violent spaces: conflict over the reappearance of Argentina's disappeared. In Schofield, J., Johnson, W.G. and Beck, C.M. (eds), *Matériel Culture: the archaeology of twentieth century conflict,* 115-31. Routledge: London and New York.

Council for British Archaeology, 2002. A review of the Defence of Britain Project. Available at: http://www.britarch.ac.uk/projects/dob/review/index.html.

Darvill, T. and Fulton, A. 1998. *The Monuments at Risk Survey of England, 1995. Main Report.* Bournemouth: School of Conservation Sciences Bournemouth University and English Heritage.

Dearing, M. 2002. Welcome to paradise: the erotic drawings of Bempton. *Illegal Media* 6, 3-7.

De Certeau, M. 1984. *The Practice of Everyday Life.* University of California Press: Los Angeles.

de la Torre, M. (ed.) 2002. *Assessing the Values of Cultural Heritage: research report,* 5-30. The Getty Conservation Institute: Los Angeles.

Dobinson, C. 1996a. *Twentieth Century Fortifications in England.* Vol. II: *Anti-Invasion Defences of World War II.* Council for British Archaeology. Unpublished report.

Dobinson, C. 1996b. *Twentieth Century Fortifications in England.* Vol. IV: *Operation Diver.* Council for British Archaeology. Unpublished report.

Dobinson, C. 1996c. *Twentieth Century Fortifications in England.* Vol. V: *Operation Overlord.* Council for British Archaeology. Unpublished report.

Dobinson, C. 2000a. *Fields of Deception: bombing decoys of World War Two*. Methuen: London.

Dobinson, C. 2000b. *Twentieth Century Fortifications in England. Supplementary Study. Experimental and Training Sites: an annotated handlist*. Council for British Archaeology. Unpublished report.

Dobinson, C. 2001. *AA Command: Britain's anti-aircraft defences of the Second World War*. Methuen: London.

Dobinson, C., Lake, J. and Schofield, J. 1997. Monuments of war: defining England's twentieth-century defence heritage. *Antiquity* 71, 288-99.

DoE, 1990. *Planning Policy Guidance Note 16: Archaeology and Planning*. HMSO: London.

Dolff-Bonekaemper, G. nd. Sites of historical significance and sites of discord: historic monuments as a tool for discussing conflict in Europe. In *Forward Planning: the function of cultural heritage in a changing Europe*, 53-7. Council of Europe.

Dolff-Bonekaemper, G. 2002a. The Berlin Wall: an archaeological site in progress. In Schofield, J., Johnson, W.G. and Beck, C.M. (eds), *Matériel Culture: the archaeology of twentieth century conflict*, 236-48. Routledge: London and New York.

Dolff-Bonekaemper, G. 2002b. Sites of hurtful memory. *Conservation* 17(2), 4-10.

Dolff-Bonekaemper, G. (co-ord.) 2005. *Dividing Lines, Connecting Lines – Europe's cross-border heritage*. Council of Europe Publishing: Strasbourg.

Douet, J. 1998. *British Barracks: their architecture and role in society*. The Stationery Office: London.

English Heritage, 1997. *Sustaining the Historic Environment: new perspectives on the future*. English Heritage: London.

English Heritage, 2000. MPP2000. *A Review of the Monuments Protection Programme 1986-2000*. English Heritage: London.

English Heritage, 2002. *Military Aircraft Crash Sites: archaeological guidance on their significance and future management*. English Heritage: London.

English Heritage, 2004a. *Military Wall Art: guidelines on its significance, conservation and management*. English Heritage: London.

English Heritage, 2004b. *The National and International Value of Bletchley Park: a platform for discussion and its future*. English Heritage. Unpublished report.

Fairclough, G. 2002. Archaeologists and the European Landscape

176

Bibliography

Convention. In Fairclough, G. and Rippon, S. (eds), *Europe's Cultural Landscape: archaeologists and the management of change*, 25-37. Europae Archaeologiae Consilium Occasional Paper 2.

Fairclough, G. 2003. Cultural landscape, sustainability, and living with change? In Teutonico, J-M. and Matero, F. (eds), *Managing Change: sustainable approaches to the conservation of the built environment*, 23-46. The Getty Conservation Institute: Los Angeles.

Fairclough, G. forthcoming. Place and locality: a non-monumental heritage. In *Proceedings of the Interpreting Historic Places conference, York (1997)*. Donhead.

Fairclough, G. and Rippon, S. (eds) 2002. *Europe's Cultural Landscape: archaeologists and the management of change*. Europae Archaeologiae Consilium Occasional Paper 2.

Feversham, P. and Schmidt, L. 1999. *The Berlin Wall Today: cultural significance and conservation issues*. Verlag Bauwesen: Berlin.

Foot, W. 1998. *The Impact of the Military on the Agricultural Landscape of Britain in the Second World War*. Unpublished MPhil thesis, University of Sussex.

Foot, W. 2003. Public archaeology: defended areas of World War II. *Conservation Bulletin* 44, 8-11.

Foot, W. 2004. *Defence Areas: a national study of Second World War anti-invasion landscapes in England*. English Heritage: London (typescript report, also available on CD-Rom).

Forty, A. 1999. Introduction. In Forty, A. and Kuchler, S. (eds), *The Art of Forgetting*, 1-18. Berg: Oxford.

Forty, A. and Kuchler, S. (eds), 1999. *The Art of Forgetting*. Berg: Oxford.

Foster, S. 1989. Analysis of spatial patterns in buildings (access analysis) as an insight into social structure: examples from the Scottish Atlantic Iron Age. *Antiquity* 63, 40-50.

Francis, P. 1996. *British Military Airfield Architecture*. Patrick Stevens: Sparkford.

Francis, P. 2003. *National Aeronautical Establishment Bedford Wind Tunnel Site*. Typescript report for English Heritage.

Furlong, J., Knight, L. and Slocombe, S. 2002. 'They shall grow not old': an analysis of trends in memorialisation based on information held by the UK National Inventory of War Memorials. *Cultural Trends* 45, 3-35.

Gaddis, J.L. 1997. *We Now Know: rethinking Cold War history*. Clarendon Press: Oxford.

Galaty, M., Stocker, S.R. and Watkinson, C. 1999. Beyond bunkers:

177

dominance, resistance and change in an Albanian regional landscape. *Journal of Mediterranean Archaeology* 12.2, 197-214.

Gane, M. 1999. Paul Virilio's bunker theorizing. *Theory, Culture and Society* 16(5), 85-102.

Gell, A. 1998. *Art and Agency: an anthropological theory.* Oxford University Press.

Geiryn T.F. 1998. Balancing Acts: Science, Enola Gay and History wars at the Smithsonian. In Macdonald S (ed.), *The Politics of Display: museums, science, culture*, 197-228. Routledge: London and New York.

Gilbert, M. 1998. *Holocaust Journey: travelling in search of the past.* Phoenix: London.

Gilchrist, R. 2003. Introduction: towards a social archaeology of warfare. *World Archaeology* 35(1), 1-6.

Gorman, A. 2005. The cultural landscape of interplanetary space. *Journal of Social Archaeology* 5(1), 85-107.

Gould, R. and Schiffer, M.B. (eds) 1981. *Modern Material Culture Studies: the archaeology of us.* Academic Press: New York.

Gould, S. 1999. Planning, development and social archaeology. In Tarlow, S. and West, S. (eds), *The Familiar Past? Archaeologies of later historical Britain*, 140-54. Routledge: London and New York.

Graves Brown, P. 1996. Road to nowhere. *Museums Journal* 96 (11), 25-7.

Graves Brown, P. (ed.) 2000. *Matter, Materiality and Modern Culture.* Routledge: London and New York.

Greer, S., Harrison, R. and McIntyre-Tamwoy, S. 2002. Community-based archaeology in Australia. *World Archaeology* 34(2), 265-87.

Groube, L. and Bowden, M. 1982. *The Archaeology of Rural Dorset, Past, Present and Future.* Dorset Natural History and Archaeology Society Monograph 4: Dorchester.

Hall, M. 2000. *Archaeology and the Modern World: colonial transcripts in South Africa and the Chesapeake.* Routledge: London and New York.

Hamilakis, Y. 2002. 'The other Parthenon': antiquity and national memory at Makronisos. *Journal of Modern Greek Studies* 20, 307-38.

Hill, P. and Wileman, J. 2002. *Landscapes of War: the archaeology of aggression and defence.* Tempus: Stroud.

Hinchliffe, R. 1997. The Cold War: the need to remember or desire to forget? *History Workshop Journal* 43, 234-9.

Bibliography

Hobsbawm, E. 1995. *Age of Extremes: the short twentieth century, 1914-91.* Abacus: London.

Holmes, R. 1997. *War Walks 2: from the Battle of Hastings to the Blitz.* BBC Books.

Holtorf, C. 2002. Is the past a non-renewable resource? In Layton, R., Stone, P. and Thomas, J. (eds), *The Destruction and Conservation of Cultural Property*, 286-97. Routledge: London and New York.

Holyoak, V. 2001. Airfields as battlefields, aircraft as an archaeological resource: British military aviation in the first half of the twentieth century. In Freeman, P. and Pollard, A. (eds), *Fields of Conflict: progress and prospect in battlefield archaeology*, 253-64. BAR International Series 958.

Holyoak, V. 2002. Out of the blue: assessing military aircraft crash sites in England, 1912-45. *Antiquity* 76, 657-63.

Holyoak, V. and Saunders, A. 2004. Who owns our dead? *British Archaeology* 75, 10-15.

Hoshower-Leppo 2002. Missing in action: searching for America's war dead. In Schofield, J., Johnson, W.G. and Beck, C.M. (eds), *Matériel Culture: the archaeology of twentieth century conflict*, 80-90. Routledge: London and New York.

Jarvis, H. 2002. Mapping Cambodia's 'killing fields'. In Schofield, J., Johnson, W.G. and Beck, C.M. (eds), *Matériel Culture: the archaeology of twentieth century conflict*, 91-102. Routledge: London and New York.

Jeffery, B. 2004. World War II shipwrecks in Truc Lagoon: the role of interest groups. *CRM: The Journal of Heritage Stewardship* 1(2), 51-67.

Johnson, W.G. and Beck, C.M. 1995. Proving ground of the nuclear age. *Archaeology* 48(3), 43-49.

Jones, D. (ed.), 2002. *20th Century Heritage: our recent cultural legacy.* Proceedings of the Australia ICOMOS National Conference 2001. School of Architecture, Landscape Architecture & Urban Design, the University of Adelaide and Australia ICOMOS Secretariat.

Joy, J. 2002. Biography of a medal: people and the things they value. In Schofield, J., Johnson, W.G. and Beck, C.M. (eds), *Matériel Culture: the archaeology of twentieth century conflict*, 132-42. Routledge: London and New York.

Keegan, J. 1993. *A History of Warfare.* London, Pimlico.

Keegan, J. 1995. *The Battle for History: re-fighting World War Two.* Hutchinson: London.

Kippin, J. 2001. *Cold War Pastoral: Greenham Common.* Black Dog Publishing Ltd: London.

Klausmeier, A. and Schmidt, L. 2004. *Wall Remnants – Wall Traces: the comprehensive guide to the Berlin Wall.* Westkreuz-Verlag: Berlin/Bonn.

Kuchler, S. 1999. The place of memory. In Forty, A. and Kuchler, S. (eds), *The Art of Forgetting*, 53-72. Berg: Oxford.

Kuletz, V.L. 1998. *The Tainted Desert: environmental and social ruin in the American West.* Routledge: New York and London.

Lacey, C. 2003. *Fireshed: the application of GIS techniques to historic military data.* Unpublished MSc dissertation, University of Southampton.

Lake, J. 2003. *Thematic Survey of Military Aviation Sites and Structures.* English Heritage: unpublished report.

Lake, J. and Schofield, J. 2000. Conservation and the Battle of Britain. In Addison, P. and Crang, J.A. (eds), *The Burning Blue: a new history of the Battle of Britain*, 229-42. Pimlico: London.

Landzelius, M. 2003. Commemorative dis(re)membering: erasing heritage, spatializing disinheritance. *Environment and Planning D: Society and Space* 21, 195-221.

Legendre, J-P. 2001. Archaeology of World War 2: the Lancaster bomber of Fléville (Meurthe-et-Moselle, France). In Buchli, V. and Lucas, G. *Archaeologies of the Contemporary Past*, 126-37. Routledge: London and New York.

Le Grange, L. 1996. The urbanism of District Six. In Anon., *The Last Days of District Six*, 7-15. The District Six Museum: Cape Town.

Linenthal, E.T. 1995. Struggling with history and memory. *Journal of American History*, December, 1094-1101.

Lowry, B. (ed.), 1995. *20th Century Defences in Britain: an introductory guide.* Council for British Archaeology Practical Handbooks in Archaeology No. 12.

MacDonald, S. 1996. *Modern Matters: principles and practice in conserving recent architecture.* English Heritage and Donhead: Shaftesbury.

Malan, A. and Soudien, C. 2002. Managing heritage in District Six, Cape Town: conflicts past and present. In Schofield, J., Johnson, W.G. and Beck, C.M. (eds), *Matériel Culture: the archaeology of twentieth century conflict*, 249-65. Routledge: London and New York.

Mason, R. 2002. Assessing values in conservation planning: methodological issues and choices. In de la Torre, M. (ed.), *Assessing the*

Bibliography

Values of Cultural Heritage: research report, 5-30. The Getty Conservation Institute: Los Angeles.

McIntyre-Tamwoy, S. 2002. Places people value: social significance and cultural exchange in post-invasion Australia. In Harrison, R. and Williamson, C. (eds), *After Captain Cook: the archaeology of the recent indigenous past in Australia*, 171-90. Sydney University Archaeological Methods Series 8.

McOmish, D., Field, D. and Brown, G. 2001. *The Field Archaeology of Salisbury Plain Training Area*. English Heritage: London.

Michelin Guide 1994 (facsimile copy of the original). *Illustrated Michelin Guides to the Battle-fields (1914-1918). The Somme: Volume 1: The First Battle of the Somme (1916-1917) (Albert, Bapaume, Peronne).* Facsimile published by G.H. Smith and Son: York.

Middleton, B. 2002. Historic environment: agri-environment schemes. *Conservation Bulletin* 42, 16-21.

Moreland, J. 2001. *Archaeology and Text*. Duckworth Debates in Archaeology: London.

Nieke, M. and Nieke, R.H. 2003. Harperley PoW Camp: memories and monuments. *Conservation Bulletin* 44, 22-5.

Noakes, L. 1997. Making histories: experiencing the Blitz in London's museums in the 1990s. In Evans, M. and Lunn, K. (eds), *War and Memory in the Twentieth Century*, 89-104. Berg: Oxford and New York.

Olivier, L. 2001. The archaeology of the contemporary past. In Buchli, V. and Lucas, G. 2001. *Archaeologies of the Contemporary Past*, 175-88. Routledge: London and New York.

Perkins, G. 1999. Museum war exhibits: propaganda or interpretation? *Interpretation* 4, 38-42.

Pritchard, C. 1999. European peace movements: rises and falls 1958-65, 1978-85 and 1990-98. In Choue, Y.S. (ed.), *World Encyclopedia of Peace*, 2nd edn, 177-81. Oceana Publications, Inc. Seoul Press.

Razac, O. 2002. *Barbed Wire: a political history* (trans from the French by Jonathan Kneight). Profile Books: London

Read, P. 1996. *Returning to Nothing: the meaning of lost places*. Cambridge University Press.

Rogers, R. 1999. *Technological Landscapes*. Royal College of Art: London.

Roseneil, S. 2000. *Common Women, Uncommon Practices: the queer feminisms of Greenham*. Cassell: London and New York.

Rugg, D.S. 1994. Communist legacies in the Albanian landscape. *Geographical Review* 84, 59-73.

Saunders, N. 2002a. Excavating memories: archaeology and the Great War, 1914-2001. *Antiquity* 76, 101-8.

Saunders, N. 2002b. The ironic 'culture of shells' in the Great War and beyond. In Schofield, J., Johnson, W.G. and Beck, C.M. (eds), *Matériel Culture: the archaeology of twentieth century conflict*, 22-40. Routledge: London and New York.

Saunders, N. (ed.), 2004. *Matters of Conflict: material culture, memory and the First World War*. Routledge: London and New York.

Saunders, R. 2002. Tell the truth: the archaeology of human rights abuses in Guatamala and the former Yugoslavia. In Schofield, J., Johnson, W.G. and Beck, C.M. (eds), *Matériel Culture: the archaeology of twentieth century conflict*, 103-114. Routledge: London and New York.

Scates, B. 2002. In Gallipoli's shadow: pilgrimage, memory, mourning and the Great War. *Australian Historic Studies* 33 (119), 1-21.

Schjeldahl, P. 1999. *Jane and Louise Wilson*. Serpentine Gallery: London.

Schmidt, L. and von Preuschen, H. (eds) 2005. *On Both Sides of the Wall: preserving monuments and sites of the Cold War era*. Westkreuz-Verlag: Berlin.

Schofield, J. 1999. Conserving recent military remains: choices and challenges for the twenty-first century. In Baker, D. and Chitty, G. (eds), *Presentation and Preservation: conflict or collaboration*, 173-86. Routledge and English Heritage: London.

Schofield, J. 2001. D-Day sites in England: an assessment. *Antiquity* 75(287), 77-83.

Schofield, J. 2002a. The role of aerial photographs in national strategic programmes: assessing recent military sites in England. In R.H. Bewley and W. Raczkowski (eds), *Aerial Archaeology: developing future practice*, 269-82. IOS Press: Amsterdam, in co-operation with NATO Scientific Affairs Division.

Schofield, J. 2002b. Monuments and the memories of war: motivations for preserving military sites in England. In Schofield, J., Johnson, W.G. and Beck, C.M. (eds), *Matériel Culture: the archaeology of twentieth century conflict*, 143-58. Routledge: London and New York.

Schofield, J. 2004. *Modern Military Matters: studying and managing the twentieth-century defence heritage in Britain: a discussion document*. Council for British Archaeology: York.

Schofield, J. in press. Jessie's cats and other stories: presenting and interpreting recent troubles. In Blockley, M. (ed.), *Heritage Interpretation*. English Heritage and Routledge: London.

Schofield, J. and Anderton, M. 2000. The queer archaeology of Green Gate: interpreting contested space at Greenham Common Airbase. *World Archaeology* 32(2), 236-51.

Schofield, J., Webster, C.J. and Anderton, M.J. 2001. Second World War remains on Black Down: a reinterpretation. *Somerset Archaeology and Natural History*, 1998, 271-86.

Schofield, J., Johnson, W.G. and Beck, C.M. (eds), 2002. *Matériel Culture: the archaeology of twentieth century conflict*. Routledge: London and New York.

Schofield, J., Beck, C.M. and Drollinger, H. 2003. The archaeology of opposition: Greenham Common and Peace Camp, Nevada. *Conservation Bulletin* 44, 47-9.

Soudien, C. and Mayer, R. nd. *The District Six Public Sculpture Project*. The District Six Museum Foundation: Cape Town.

Startin, B. 1993. Assessment of field remains. In Hunter, J. and Ralston, I. (eds), *Archaeological Resource Management in the UK: an introduction*. Alan Sutton/IFA: Stroud.

Stone, M. 2004. A memory in ruins? *Public Archaeology* 3(3), 131-44.

Symmons Roberts, M. 2001. *Burning Babylon*. Cape Poetry: London.

Szpenowski, P. 2002. Before and after The Change: the socio-economic transition period and its impact on the agriculture and cultural landscape of Poland. In Fairclough, G. and Rippon, S. (eds) 2002. *Europe's Cultural Landscape: archaeologists and the management of change*, 125-32. Europae Archaeologiae Consilium Occasional Paper 2.

Tarlow, S. 1997. An archaeology of remembering: death, bereavement and the First World War. *Cambridge Archaeological Journal* 7(1), 105-21.

Thomas, R.J.C. 2003. PoW camps: what survives and where. *Conservation Bulletin* 44, 18-21.

Tilden, F. 1957. *Interpreting our Heritage*. University of North Carolina Press: Chapel Hill.

Tuck, C., Cocroft, W.D. and McOmish, D. 2004. *Spadeadam Rocket Establishment Cumbria*. English Heritage: Archaeological Investigation Report Series AI/20/2004.

Tunbridge, J.E. and Ashworth, G.J. 1996. *Dissonant Heritage: the management of the past as a resource in conflict*. John Wiley: Chichester.

Uzzell, D. 1989. The hot interpretation of war and conflict. In Uzzell,

D. (ed.), *Heritage Interpretation*, Vol. 1: *The natural and built environment*, 33-47. Belhaven Press: London and New York.

Uzzell, D. 1998. The hot interpretation of the Cold War. In English Heritage, *Monuments of War: the evaluation, recording and management of twentieth-century military sites*, 18-21. English Heritage, London.

Uzzell, D. and Ballantyne, R. 1999. Heritage that hurts: interpretation in a postmodern world. In Uzzell, D. and Ballantyne, R. (eds), *Contemporary Issues in Heritage and Environmental Interpretation: problems and prospects*, 152-71. The Stationery Office: London.

Vermeule, E. 1996. Archaeology and philology: the dirt and the word. *Transactions of the American Philological Association* 126, 1-10.

Virilio, P. 1989. *War and Cinema: the logistics of perception*. Verso: London.

Virilio, P. 1991 [1975]. *Bunker Archeology* (trans from the French by George Collins). Les Editions du Demi-Cercle: Paris.

Virilio, P. 2002. *Desert Screen: war at the speed of light* (trans from the French by Michael Degener). Continuum: London and New York.

Virilio, P. and Lotringer, S. 1997. *Pure War* (revised edn). Semiotext(e): New York.

Watson, F. 2004. *The Hush House: Cold War sites in England*. Hush House Publishers.

Weinberg, J. and Elieli, R. 1995. *The Holocaust Museum in Washington*. Rizzoli: New York.

Walley, F. 2001. From bomb shelters to postwar buildings: 40 years' work as a civil engineer in government. *The Structural Engineer* 79(4), 15-21.

Wills, H. 1985. *Pillboxes: a study of UK defences 1940*. Leo Cooper: London.

Wilson, L.K. 2003. *Spadeadam* (film, privately distributed).

Wilson, L.K. in press. Out to the Waste: Spadeadam and the Cold War. In Schofield, J. and Cocroft, W.D. (eds), *A Fearsome Heritage: the diverse legacies of the Cold War*. UCL.

Wilson, E.O. 2001 [1998]. Consilience: the unity of knowledge. Abacus: London.

Winter, J. 1995. *Sites of Memory, Sites of Mourning: the Great War in European cultural history*. Cambridge University Press.

Index

Index

Galaty, Michael et al., 109-10
Gallipoli, 96, 107
GAMA, *see* Greenham Common
GAMMA, 78
'ghosts of place', 55, 89, 90, 107, 158, 171
Gilbert, Martin, 107, 157-8, 170
GIS, 58, 59-60, 128
Golding, William, 18
graffiti, 76, 105
Graves Brown, Paul, 29, 116, 153
Great War, the, *see* World War I
Greek Civil War, 112
Greenham Common (Berks.), 26, 29, 78-9, 121-7, 132, 143-4, 145, 148, 149, 155, 166-8
  peace camps at, 29, 100-1
  Peace Garden, 167

Hamilakis, Yannis, 112-13
hangars, 52, 55
Hardened Aircraft Shelters, 141-4
Harperley PoW camp (Co. Durham), 33, 132-3
heritage legislation, 115
Heritage Lottery Fund, 38, 120
heritage management, 10, 14, 15, 116-20
'heritage that hurts', 16, 111
Hiroshima (Japan), 26, 101, 138, 156, 169
historical sources, 14, 18, 32, 34, 35, 37, 38, 39, 40, 55, 65, 70-3, 80, 82, 83, 84
historical geography, 14
HMS Belfast, 63
Hobsbawm, Eric, 17
Holocaust Journey, 107, 157-8
holocaust museums, *see* museums
holocaust sites, 89, 94, 97, 107, 156
Holtorf, Cornelius, 116
Holyoak, Vince, 64, 66
Hornchurch (Essex), 137

'hot' interpretation, 96, 102, 152-5
Hull (East Yorks.), 33
Hunt, David, 59, 91

ICOMOS, 119, 120
Imperial War Museum, 63, 66, 99, 157, 167
  Blitz Experience at, 159-61, 170
importance, *see* value
industry, 53
INF Treaty, 126
In Flanders Field Museum (Ypres), 45, 157
information technology, 28
informed conservation, 87, 139-40
in situ preservation, 130-41
intangible heritage, 43, 89-92
intercontinental ballistic missiles, 23
internet technology, 18
interpretation, 10, 29, 152-71
Iraq, 46
Iron Curtain, 51
Ironside, General, 59

Jarvis, Helen, 104
Joy, Jody, 67, 97

Khmer Rouge, 104
Kippin, John, 79
Kirkland Air Force Base (US), 50
Korean War, 61
Kuchler, Susan, 93
Kuletz, Valerie, 48-50
Kyriakides, Yannis, 79

Lacey, Colin, 58-60
Lancaster bomber, 98
landscape, 43-51, 58-60, 89, 92, 98, 128
  bomber, 44
  historic, 91
  industrial, 48, 128

188

Index